A TABLE
SET FOR
SISTERHOOD

35 Recipes Inspired by 35 Female Icons

ASHLEY SCHÜTZ & ASHLY JERNIGAN

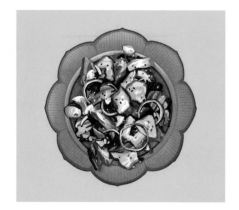

Published by Sourcebooks
P.O. Box 4410, Naperville, Illinois 60567-4410
(630) 961-3900
sourcebooks.com

Cataloging-in-Publication Data is on file with the Library of Congress.

Printed and bound in the United States of America.
WOZ 10 9 8 7 6 5 4 3 2

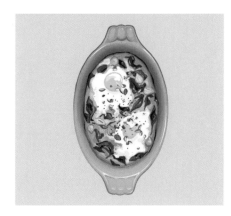

To all the women who set this table before we ever arrived.

And to all the women who haven't yet found their seat.

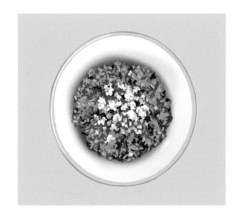

Table of Contents

Savory Recipes

Sweet Recipes

BUFFY SAINTE-MARIE

CANADA, 1941–

> "I'm trying to scatter what I can of beauty in the places I think need it, to get rid of the boredom and the meanness in the world."

As a little girl, Buffy Sainte-Marie made rubber bands disappear—rubber bands, pots, pans, *anything that made noise*. She made music, and in making music, she found her voice. By age three, she was banging out chords on the piano, blowing on blades of grass to make them shriek. At sixteen, she taught herself guitar and invented thirty-two new ways to tune her instrument, creating completely unique sounds that paired beautifully with her distinct vocals. She became a force to be reckoned with, a potent voice for Indigenous peoples.

At twenty-three, Buffy saw the UK release of her first album, *It's My Way!* Outside the folk community, it got little press, but within the folk community, it made waves. The first single, "Now That the Buffalo's Gone," lamented the ongoing injustices of European colonization, an important and deep-rooted theme throughout her music and career.

Within a year of that first album release, Buffy found herself with more money than she knew what to do with. And so, she gave back to her people, setting up a scholarship called the Nihewan Foundation for American Indian Education. "My biggest honor was to find out that two of my early scholarship recipients had gone on to found tribal colleges. Can you imagine that kind of thrill?"

She's always been an iconoclast. During the tumult of the 1960s, the world embraced her antiwar anthem, "Universal Soldier." She breastfed her son on national TV in the late 1970s—the first person to do so, and on a children's show, no less. As a recurring character on *Sesame Street*, she transformed how children learned about Native Americans. Before racism and stereotyping ever had a chance to set in, Buffy was there, telling our kids, *Hey, look at me. We're not so different. We're the same people, you and I.*

She was often silenced and blacklisted for speaking these truths. Throughout the 1960s and '70s, many radio stations in the United States suppressed her music due to "controversial" ideas about environmentalism and Indigenous rights. Regardless, Buffy never stopped breaking ground and uniting minds. Over the decades, her music relentlessly called the world to action, teaching us what an activist is and how we can take part in change. Sometimes, she reminded us, making a difference is as simple as sharing our truths: "Some people say I was very brave, but I really just didn't know any better. All I had was my originality."

Green Goddess Salad

YIELD: 4–6 SERVINGS

Green: The color of renewal, of healing, of the earth itself.
Goddess: A woman of superhuman influence, a creator.

The book you hold in your hands is full of goddesses—women who go beyond the normal scope of achievement. All our feisty feminists deserve the title, but we matched Buffy Sainte-Marie with this green, nutrient-packed recipe for a couple of reasons.

First, Buffy is a protector. She fights to preserve the verdant spaces of the world. As we listened to "I'm Gonna Be a Country Girl Again," one line struck us about how the lights on

Buffy Sainte-Marie

Broadway wouldn't amount to an acre of green. It's true, after all: human beings aren't born out of cities—they're born out of the green earth, the land we inherit from our ancestors.

Second, Buffy's music, message, and voice are timeless but also adaptable—superhumanly so. She's a force of nature, comfortable wherever she finds herself, with a guitar tuned any one of thirty-two ways.

We like to think of our dressing the same way: it can be an appetizer dip or a marinade for roast chicken. Experiment a bit, and we bet you'll find thirty more pairings that work just as well!

GREEN GODDESS DRESSING

¼ cup mayonnaise or the flesh of half an avocado
2 tablespoons champagne vinegar or a mild white wine vinegar
1 clove fresh garlic, minced
Zest and juice of 1 lemon
1 ¼ cups flat-leaf parsley leaves and fine stems
½ cup basil leaves
¼ cup dill (and/or tarragon) leaves, plus extra for garnish
2 tablespoons chopped chives, plus extra for garnish
½ cup grape-seed oil or another mild oil
1 teaspoon sea salt, plus more to taste
Freshly cracked black pepper

- Combine the mayonnaise (or avocado), vinegar, garlic, and lemon zest and juice in a high-powered blender. Blend for a moment just to combine.

- Add the green herbs to the blender, followed by the oil, salt, and pepper. Blend until well combined. This dressing can be as smooth or as chunky as you like. We err on the side of a creamy pesto-like consistency. Taste the dressing for balance by dunking in a slice of cucumber or leaf of lettuce. Add more acid, salt, oil, or mayonnaise (or avocado) as you see fit. Set aside while preparing the salad.

SALAD

2 heads romaine lettuce or 4 small heads little gems lettuce
3 Persian cucumbers or ½ English cucumber
5 to 6 radishes
Flaky salt to finish

- Slice the lettuce (romaine or little gem) in half and then in quarters (or more) from root to tip. Dunk into a bowl of cold water to clean, and then dry well in a salad spinner. We love this salad as a "fork and knife" salad, but if you prefer smaller lettuce pieces, feel free to slice or tear as you like.

- Wash the cucumbers and radishes well, and thinly slice into coins or half moons.

- Plate the salad greens, followed by a generous drizzle of Green Goddess Dressing and a scatter of cucumber and radish slices. Finish off with flaky salt and a few rough chops of dill (and/or tarragon if using) and chives for garnish.

RECIPE PAIRING IDEA

The Green Goddess Salad shines as the perfect accessory to any meal. We particularly love it at the table with Tawakkol Karman's Roasted Eggplant with Fried Lamb and Zhoug (page 110) or alongside Gloria Steinem's Caramelized Fennel Pasta (page 98).

The Question at the Table

When have you been silenced or told to lower your voice when you spoke about something important to you?

Buffy Sainte-Marie

LEYMAH GBOWEE

LIBERIA, 1972–

"Be bold. Step out and never walk on tiptoes. Those who walk on tiptoes can never leave footprints for people to walk in."

Nudity is not often used as a weapon, and reason says we should be skeptical of anyone who threatens to use it as a weapon!

Except Leymah Gbowee. In 2003, the Liberian activist led a delegation to Accra, Ghana, to take part in talks with President Charles Taylor, a war criminal who had sustained a state of war for fourteen years. When the peace negotiations stalled, Leymah and some two hundred Christian and Muslim women used their own bodies as a barricade, preventing Taylor and his men from leaving the meeting hall until they agreed to a peace settlement. Security forces attempted to arrest Leymah, whereupon she made one of the gutsiest moves in the history of protest.

She threatened to disrobe.

It may sound odd to some of us, but it was an act of genius. According to the traditional beliefs of that region, seeing a married or elderly woman purposefully bare herself is tantamount to a curse.

The act turned the tides of the peace talks, ushering in the official end of war and Taylor's resignation and exile. It also paved the way for the 2005 election of Ellen Johnson Sirleaf as president of Liberia, the first free and democratically elected female leader of an African country. Leymah went on to share the 2011 Nobel Peace Prize with Sirleaf and Tawakkol Karman (also featured in these pages).

Peace would have been impossible without the cooperation of both Christian and Muslim women, who united despite their differences to protest and ensure a brighter future for Liberia. In 2006, Leymah cofounded the Women Peace and Security Network Africa, working to promote African women's roles in government, pushing for peace and security for people regardless of their faith.

For the last decade and more, Leymah has turned her gaze to young women in order to reverse generations of marginalization and abuse. "When these girls sit, you unlock intelligence," she said of these efforts. "You unlock passion. You unlock commitment. You unlock focus. You unlock great leaders."

Mothers, daughters, sisters, grandmothers, aunts, caretakers—pause a moment to look at these little girls under your care. Cook with them. Read with them. Show them the world Leymah imagines.

Spice Roasted Sweet Potatoes with Yogurt and Cilantro

YIELD: 4–6 SERVINGS

We hope to honor some of the staple flavors of West Africa—those flavors closest to Leymah's heart. At the same time, we wanted to create something complex to honor the fantastically diverse history of the continent: its culinary traditions, its cultures, its stories.

Sweet potatoes, originally from Central and South America, are a staple ingredient in Liberia, where both the roots and greens are used widely. We coated the root's beautiful orange flesh in a Scotch bonnet (West Africa's chili of choice, but if you can't find it, then feel free to substitute with another hot chili pepper!), coriander, and brown sugar marinade. Flavor

Leymah Gbowee

balance is achieved with a dollop of tangy yogurt, lots of juicy pomegranate seeds, and full leaves of fresh cilantro. You will likely *love* this marinade, so consider doubling the recipe and marinating everything from chicken to salmon, shrimp, zucchini, and so much more! Feel free to get playful with changing out the citrus or the seeds here too, maybe even using fresh dill or opal basil instead of cilantro!

The outcome is wildly colorful, bright with delicious diversity—just like the women of Liberia who are uniting for peace as you read these words. Think of them as you cook and as you eat.

CHILI MARINADE

¼ cup olive oil

¼ cup brown sugar

1 green onion, white and light green parts sliced

1 Scotch bonnet pepper (or other hot chili pepper), seeded

1 tablespoon soy sauce

1 tablespoon freshly cracked black pepper

2 teaspoons sea salt

1 teaspoon ground coriander

½ teaspoon ground allspice (or ¼ teaspoon each cloves and cinnamon)

½ teaspoon ground ginger

Zest of 1 lime

- Combine all the ingredients in a food processor or blender, and blend until combined. Set aside in a medium-sized bowl.

SWEET POTATOES

3 pounds sweet potatoes, scrubbed and cut into 1 ½-inch cubes

2 cups whole milk Greek yogurt

½ bunch fresh cilantro, leaves picked

¾ cup pomegranate seeds

½ cup pumpkin seeds, toasted

Good olive oil for drizzling

Half a lime

Flaky salt and freshly cracked black pepper

- Preheat the oven to 400°F, and line a sheet tray with parchment paper.

Leymah Gbowee

- Add the cubed sweet potatoes to the bowl with the marinade, and toss to combine.

- Spread the sweet potatoes out on the prepared sheet tray, and roast for 25 to 35 minutes, until tender and browned on the edges. Let cool for 5 minutes.

- Place the roasted sweet potatoes in a low serving bowl. Top with large spoonfuls of yogurt, followed by heavy sprinkles of cilantro leaves, pomegranate seeds, and pumpkin seeds. Drizzle with olive oil, squeeze the lime onto the pile, and sprinkle flaky salt and ground pepper before serving.

RECIPE PAIRING IDEA

This dish can easily be a meal in itself, but if you'd like to invite other flavors (and stories) to the table with that same spice-rich note, then may we recommend pairing with Malala Yousafzai's Cardamom Spiced Roasted Chicken (page 130) and Angela Davis's Spiced Molasses Cake with Crunchy Lemon Glaze (page 170) for a table truly set for sisterhood?

The Question at the Table

What is one way in which you could actively create more peace in a situation currently causing you stress or unrest?

RUTH COKER BURKS

USA, 1959–

"I knew that what I was doing was right, and I knew that I was doing what God asked me. It wasn't a voice from the sky. I knew deep in my soul."

In 1984, while visiting a friend in the hospital, Arkansas native Ruth Coker Burks noticed hospital staff avoiding a particular room. The door was covered with red plastic.

Ruth learned the young man inside was dying of a then relatively unknown disease: gay-related immune deficiency, or GRID—what would later become known as AIDS. She came to know Jimmy, whose family declined to care for him, and she took over his care, turning the coldness of his hospital room into a place of love and acceptance. On the day of his passing, Ruth stayed with him for thirteen hours. His mother had refused to come say goodbye.

"I went back in his room," Ruth said. "And when I walked in, he said, 'Oh, momma. I knew you'd come,' and then he lifted his hand. And what was I going to do? What was I going to do? So I took his hand. I said, 'I'm here, honey. I'm here.'"

She found a funeral home to accept his remains and buried his ashes in her own family cemetery.

These were not small acts, especially in a time when the public knew little about AIDS, when so many refused the suffering of others, denying them personhood when they were most afraid and alone. Still, this was only the beginning.

Ruth began receiving calls from other AIDS sufferers. She took patients to appointments, stockpiled medications, and applied for financial assistance, operating with such compassion and efficiency that those in her care lived longer than other AIDS patients of the time.

More than this: Ruth became family to the dying.

Over the decades of her advocacy, Ruth became a pivotal member of the AIDS care and gay rights movement: she served as a White House consultant for AIDS education and attracted the attention of major disease-fighting organizations, which sent researchers to investigate her methods.

Thankfully, AIDS care has improved throughout the world, but there are still those in need—from this disease and a thousand other crises.

You might help them. *You* might become someone's family. All it takes is a willingness to step through that door, to introduce yourself to your neighbor, to reach out to someone a world away—to say, *I'm here.*

Rainbow Salad

YIELD: 4–6 SERVINGS

Ruth Coker Burks was a friend, sister, aunt, and mother to those abandoned by their own. During their final and most difficult days, she showed kindness, tenderness, inclusion, and love—the feelings they most craved and deserved. She was a beacon of acceptance in a world still struggling with fear and hatred.

But lest we risk coloring this with too much darkness, one thing we tend to miss when we mourn the victims of the AIDS crisis is this...

Gay spaces have always been defined by joy—an ecstatic, defiant-in-the-face-of-tragedy joy. Even during the worst periods of the crisis, gay men celebrated their identities. Ruth, who received financial assistance and support from gay bars in Arkansas, knew this and

adopted it in her own life. The joyous rainbow flag that she celebrated inspires this recipe. Eclectic and diverse ingredients make up our LGBTQ+ communities just as surely as they make up this salad.

TAHINI TURMERIC MAPLE DRESSING

¼ cup olive oil

¼ cup tahini

2 tablespoons apple cider vinegar

2 tablespoons maple syrup

1 tablespoon Dijon mustard

1 tablespoon lime juice

¼ teaspoon ground turmeric

⅛ teaspoon ground cayenne pepper

Flaky salt and freshly cracked black pepper to taste

Water, as needed

- Combine all the ingredients except the water in a blender. Blend until well emulsified. Check for flavor balance and texture. Some brands of tahini can seize up and thicken more than others. Add water 1 tablespoon at a time to achieve desired consistency. The goal is a salad dressing that is voluminous but not as thick as mayonnaise.

NOTE: *Another great way to use this salad dressing is to make it a dip for raw veggies (cucumber, fennel, radishes, and rainbow carrots). Simply omit the apple cider vinegar and water. If you need to thicken it more (to the texture of hummus), add 1 more tablespoon of tahini and maple syrup, plus 1 teaspoon of Dijon mustard. Check for flavor balance.*

SALAD

1 (15-ounce) can garbanzo beans, rinsed and drained

2 pounds winter squash (kabocha is our favorite)

2 tablespoons olive oil

Flaky salt and freshly cracked black pepper to taste

1 semi-firm pear, thinly sliced

2 cups red cabbage or radicchio, thinly sliced

2 to 3 rainbow carrots, thinly sliced into circles

¼ cup each mint and basil leaves, torn roughly

- Preheat the oven to 350°F.

- Line a sheet tray or rimmed dish with a clean kitchen towel. Pour the drained garbanzo beans on top, spread into a single layer, and allow to dry for 15 to 30 minutes (the drier they are, the crispier they become). Don't skip this step!

- Cut the winter squash in half, and spoon out the seeds. Lay the cut side on the cutting board for stability, and peel away the tough exterior with a sharp knife or vegetable peeler. Cut the firm orange flesh into 2-inch chunks about ½ inch thick, and spread out on a sheet tray lined with parchment paper.

- Scatter the garbanzo beans over the squash, drizzle with olive oil, and sprinkle with salt and pepper. Roast in the oven for 20 minutes, stirring once halfway through. The squash should be cooked through, and the beans will be golden brown. Let cool for at least 5 minutes on the pan after baking.

- Combine the cooled roasted squash and beans with the pear, sliced cabbage, and carrots in a large bowl. Drizzle the dressing over a spoonful at a time, tossing lightly and tasting for flavor balance, adding more dressing, salt, and pepper as needed.

- Pile the salad onto a large platter, and top with torn herbs.

RECIPE PAIRING IDEA

This beautiful salad would love to buddy up next to any of our other dishes, but may we recommend accompanying Irena Sendler's Garlicky Breadcrumbs with Broccoli and Feta (page 44) or Sampat Pal Devi's Beet Risotto with Hazelnuts (page 94)?

The Question at the Table

Who taught you the most about kindness or generosity,
and what did you learn from them?

QIU JIN

CHINA, 1875–1907

"With all my heart, I beseech and beg my two hundred million female compatriots to assume their responsibility as citizens. Arise! Arise! Chinese women, arise!"

Listen. When your bio includes the words *enjoyed wine, swords, and making bombs*, you shouldn't be referred to as "China's Joan of Arc." Screw that imperialist noise—Joan of Arc is France's Qiu Jin.

Qiu Jin (pronounced "chee-o jean") lived a mere thirty-one years before being publicly beheaded in 1907, but three decades was more than enough time to inspire generations. Through poetry, she celebrated those women—often forgotten, rarely given their due—whose heroism helped shape China. By 1903, she was advocating vocally for women's rights and an end to foot binding and arranged marriages.

If all that sounds squeaky clean, hear this: two years later, Qiu Jin joined the Triads, a secret society and criminal organization involved in the overthrow of the Qing Dynasty. Just before her execution, Qiu Jin was named head of the Datong girls' school, which trained revolutionaries in secret.

Though she died without seeing the revolution she fought so hard for, Qiu Jin's death caught the attention of other revolutionaries, bringing much-needed change to Chinese society. To this day, she remains one of East Asia's most celebrated feminists.

Lemony Smashed Cucumber Salad

YIELD: 4–6 SERVINGS

Food culture is rooted in place and time: the same ingredient can grow in hundreds of different countries and climates without ever being prepared the exact same way. Recipes are also stories, allegories. Try this one.

A traditional Chinese method of preparing cucumber is to smash it, *hard*, with a heavy pan, a rolling pin, a sword—whatever you've got! Breaking and bruising the cucumber allows it to better absorb other ingredients. Qiu Jin smashed through barriers. The Qing Dynasty ultimately broke her, but not before her words and actions had been absorbed by the people of China.

"Arise! Chinese women, arise!"

They did, their mouths formed into shouts, their fists clenched around panhandles, around rolling pins—around swords.

Arise!

RECIPE

6 Persian cucumbers or 2 English cucumbers
1 red onion
2 medium lemons
2 tablespoons rice wine vinegar
1 tablespoon sugar
½ teaspoon sea salt, plus a pinch
1 teaspoon fish sauce
2 tablespoons sesame oil

1 tablespoon neutral oil
¼ teaspoon crushed red pepper flakes, or more to taste
2 tablespoons toasted sesame seeds
Freshly cracked black pepper

- Wash and trim the ends off each cucumber. Use a rolling pin or the bottom of a heavy pan to smash each cucumber a few times until it splits in various places. Use your hands to break off multiple craggy, geode-like bits of cucumber (about 1- to 2-inch pieces). Set all the smashed cucumber bits into a colander to drain off any liquid.

- Slice the red onion into thin half moons, just thick enough to still provide a crunch. Place the slices in a bowl of ice water for 10 minutes to take the spicy edge off. Then drain and set aside.

- Halve one lemon lengthwise, and remove the pithy tips of the top and bottom. Halve those halves lengthwise again, leaving you with 4 long wedges. Slice crosswise into thin quarter moons—skin, pith, pulp, and all! Be cautious to remove seeds as they come up against the knife. Set the lemon slices in a small bowl, and sprinkle with a generous pinch of salt. Mix with your hands, giving the lemon slices a slight massage, and set aside to marinate for 10 minutes.

- Combine the zest and juice of the other lemon in a large bowl with the rice wine vinegar, sugar, salt, and fish sauce. Whisk to encourage the sugar to dissolve. Whisk in the two oils.

- Discard any water from the smashed cucumbers before adding the cucumber to the bowl of dressing. Top with red pepper flakes, sesame seeds, cracked pepper, salted lemons, and the chilled red onions. Fold all the ingredients together, and taste for flavor balance. Since all cucumbers vary slightly in size, it's important to pay attention to what *your* salad still needs here. More spice? Add more red pepper flakes. More salt? Add another pinch of salt. More sweet? Add a bit more sugar. More umami? Add a dash of fish sauce or sesame oil. More acid? Add more lemon juice or vinegar.

Qiu Jin

NOTE: *This recipe is best when enjoyed just after combining all the ingredients together. If the cucumber is seasoned too early, it can get a little slimy in texture. This salad is crunchy and bright, so best to honor those qualities and toss it together just as guests are sitting at the table. You can smash the cucumber and make the salted lemons, onion, and dressing up to 2 days in advance and hold separately.*

RECIPE PAIRING IDEA

This salad would make a perfect pairing alongside Junko Tabei's Bold Peanutty Shrimp (page 118) or Malala Yousafzai's Cardamom Spiced Roasted Chicken (page 130), but feel free to smash up these cucumbers and ready them for nearly any meal!

The Question at the Table

Just as Qiu Jin is often referred to as "China's Joan of Arc," what influential contemporary or figure from the past would you like to be compared to?

WANGARI MAATHAI

KENYA, 1940–2011

> "Finally I was able to see that if I had
> a contribution I wanted to make, I
> must do it, despite what others said.
> That I was OK the way I was. That
> it was all right to be strong."

There are many ways to be awesome. You could be the best painter, the best winemaker, the best physicist, the best parent or sister or aunt.

Or you could be the first woman to earn a PhD in your country, the first woman from your continent to receive a Nobel Prize, and the first woman to combat deforestation in sub-Saharan Africa on a grand scale.

Oh, wait, you can't do those things, because Wangari Muta Maathai already did! (Don't worry though. I bet you're awesome in a bunch of other ways.) For seven decades, Wangari stood up to everything in her way—a husband, a country, private landowners—in order to restore what had been lost to deforestation in her native Kenya.

By thirty-one, she was already nearly a legend, overcoming prejudice to become the first East African woman to receive a PhD. She fought for greater gender equity in her university, first as a student and then as a professor. In her mid to late thirties, she turned her whole attention to reforestation. By 1977, she had created the Green Belt Movement, which focused on native tree planting, environmental conservation, and women's rights issues. She was arrested and detained more than once, politicians attempted to criminalize her and other Green Belt Movement members' actions, and for a while, she was forced into hiding.

Nonetheless, she persisted. She did this as a single woman, raising multiple children: she and her husband had divorced in 1979. The husband's argument? Wangari was "too educated, too strong, too successful, too stubborn, and too hard to control."

Damn right she was. To date, the Green Belt Movement has planted over fifty-one million trees. Over thirty thousand women have been trained in sustainable forestry, food preparation, beekeeping, and other skills that generate income without damaging the land. In 2004, Wangari received the Nobel Peace Prize—the first African woman and the first environmentalist to do so.

Celery Root and Pecan Salad

YIELD: 4–6 SERVINGS

Wangari Maathai loved her country dearly. She worked to restore her land but also looked toward a sustainable future for all of us. Without the conservation of our soil, how can we grow? You plant a tree, and its roots sink deep into the earth, gripping rocks and dirt, preventing erosion, and making it possible for even more to grow.

Speaking of roots...the modest celery root is the star of the show here. If you're lucky enough to buy one freshly picked, it'll come in a tangle, crusted in rich dirt. At first ugly—a mystery of a vegetable to most—it provides a slightly sweet, earthy, and delightfully crunchy flavor. For this recipe, the root stays in all its raw glory but is coated in vinaigrette, toasted pecans, and peppery greens.

The root is the standout ingredient the world didn't know it needed! Just like Wangari.

RECIPE

2 tablespoons finely chopped shallots
¼ cup champagne vinegar (or quality white wine vinegar)
Juice of ½ lemon
⅔ cup olive oil
½ teaspoon sea salt, plus more to taste
Freshly cracked black pepper
1 medium celery root, peeled
¾ cup toasted, chopped pecans
¼ cup chopped Italian flat-leaf parsley
A healthy mix of arugula, cress, mâche, or other vibrant greens

Wangari Maathai

- Place the shallots in the base of a blender, and cover with the vinegar and lemon juice. Allow to sit for 10 minutes in the blender before adding any more ingredients (this helps take the oniony edge off the shallots—pro tip!).

- Add the olive oil, salt, and pepper to the blender, and blend on high speed until emulsified.

- Grate the peeled celery root on the large grate of a standing cheese grater, and put in a medium bowl. Add the chopped pecans and parsley.

- Line a beautiful platter or individual salad plates with greens. Add the salad dressing to the grated celery root mixture, toss, and taste for seasoning. Add more salt and pepper if necessary. Pile the celery root mixture over the greens, and drizzle a touch more olive oil over any exposed greens.

- It is best to eat this salad right after dressing it.

RECIPE PAIRING IDEA

This is a comfort salad you'll want alongside every meal. No, really! It's simple to throw together and goes well with everything. But we will say, you pair this salad with Brenda Berkman's Pork Winter Squash Ragù (page 104) or RBG's Smashed Potatoes with Crème Fraîche and Caviar (page 56), and you really will have struck gold at the dinner table.

The Question at the Table

Trees reach low into the ground and high into the sky. Today,
what was your high, and what was your low?

Wangari Maathai

GRETA THUNBERG

SWEDEN, 2003–

> "You say you love your children above all else, and yet you are stealing their future in front of their very eyes."

Reason says that in a country privileged with resources to provide for most of its citizens, an average teenager should be thinking about anything other than the destruction of the world.

Two things:

1. Greta Thunberg was no average teenager when she started this fight.

2. If the world is to be saved from the catastrophic effects of climate change, who better to force us out of our lassitude than a brilliant and informed *young* woman—the very face of our species' future?

If she has somehow escaped your notice, Greta Thunberg is a Swedish climate activist. She rose to international fame in August 2018 (at the age of fifteen) after sitting in front of the Swedish parliament for three straight weeks, skipping school in protest of world leaders' inaction on climate change. Her country had just been through its hottest summer in over 250 years, suffering numerous heat waves and wildfires.

She continued to strike on Fridays as the hashtags #FridaysForFuture and #ClimateStrike trended globally. Students from around the world began their own strikes. By the end of 2018, over twenty thousand students had organized strikes in at least 270 cities.

Greta has made enemies, especially among the conservative media. It's not hard to see why:

she has placed the blame solely where it lies—with her elders, with those who remain more concerned with making money than ensuring a healthy world for those who follow.

Should an adolescent have enemies around the world? No. Of course not. But heroes like Greta keep their eyes fixed forward; they look to a better world and denounce those who stand in the way of its realization. They are courageous, unafraid in the face of anyone's scorn. Let us take a moment, together, to read her words. Let us imagine our own daughters standing before world leaders, speaking truth to power as Greta did during the 2019 UN Climate Action Summit:

"People are suffering. People are dying. Entire ecosystems are collapsing. We are in the beginning of a mass extinction. And all you can talk about is money and fairy tales of eternal economic growth. How dare you... You are failing us. But the young people are starting to understand your betrayal. The eyes of all future generations are upon you. And if you choose to fail us, I say: We will never forgive you."

Cashew Chipotle Dip

YIELD: 2 ½ CUPS

Look, Greta is incredible, an example of what one dedicated individual can accomplish, but she's also startlingly aware of her own place in history. She knows she's not the solution. She knows how much work is ahead of us. All of us, together.

The important thing is that a serious discussion is taking place. And these discussions, large and small, do equal change. That change is different for everyone. It may take the shape of direct political activism, lifestyle changes, or simply a greater emphasis on awareness—looking at your community with eyes wide open. Over time, our priorities will change.

We made this recipe for Greta for the main reason that dips are something you make for a crowd, whether you intend to sit around your table discussing great women of the world or packing for your journey to the next #FridaysForFuture sit-in.

Whatever your plans, this a conversation food. So keep the conversation going!

RECIPE

3 cups raw cashews
1 to 3 whole chipotles in adobo sauce
1 ½ teaspoons sea salt
1 tablespoon apple cider vinegar
1 tablespoon lemon juice
2 teaspoons maple syrup
¾ cup cold water (or more as needed)

- Place the cashews, desired amount of chipotles (or start with 1 and work up from there), salt, apple cider vinegar, lemon juice, maple syrup, and half the water in the bowl of a food processor or high-powered blender, and start the machine. Add the rest of the water slowly as the nuts begin to break down with the motor running until it is a nice hummus-like consistency. Taste and adjust as needed: more water if it's too thick, more salt or lemon juice if it needs more savory or punch. Keep in mind that the flavors will develop as it sits, along with the thickness.

- Holds well in a covered container for up to 7 days.

NOTE: *These measurements are more of a guide than a hard and fast rule. It is important to taste and adjust this dip as you make it. Too spicy? Add more maple syrup. Too flat? Add more acidity with vinegar or lemon juice.*

RECIPE PAIRING IDEA

Basically, you can bring Greta's Cashew Chipotle Dip to any and all dinner parties from here on out. Serve it alongside Rupi Kaur's Summer Shrub (page 208) and the Mirabal Sisters' Sweet, Salty, and Spicy Popcorn (page 166) for a really delicious appetizer spread that will get people talking.

The Question at the Table

If you had to choose just one social issue to stand for, what would it be?

ALEXANDRIA OCASIO-CORTEZ

USA, 1989–

"They'll tell you you're too loud, that you need to wait your turn and ask the right people for permission. Do it anyway."

The first thing you need to understand about Alexandria Ocasio-Cortez (affectionately known as AOC) is that she embodies ambition. The second thing you need to understand is that the very word *ambition* is used as a weapon against her—as if a woman is immediately suspect if she wants to influence the world around her the way men do. People who think this way don't like to hear about the work she's put in, the resistance she's faced, and they sure as hell don't like hearing what she's accomplished.

But we're not those people, so let's hear the good news! On June 26, 2018, AOC drew national recognition when she won the Democratic Party's primary election for New York's 14th congressional district and became the youngest woman in American history to be elected to Congress.

She represents her community and the American people by fighting alongside them. She sees the need for serious change and actually proposes solutions big enough to match the crises we are facing today. AOC has spearheaded legislation impacting the dire needs of our suffering planet while acknowledging the class imbalances that affect us most.

The journey hasn't been *easy*, obviously. AOC is still held to a higher standard than the men around her. Recall that moment when the 45th sitting president of the U.S. told her and the other women of color claiming seats of Congress to, and we quote, "Go back and help fix the totally broken and crime-infested places from which they came." AOC clapped right back, stating, "Mr. President, the country I 'come from,' & the country we all swear to, is the United States."

Or how about when she was verbally attacked by Congressman Ted Yoho? She followed it up with a powerful, ceiling-shattering speech that stabbed a hot poker at toxic misogyny. Her message was clear: just because a man has a daughter or a wife, it does not make him *decent*. In her words, "Treating people with dignity and respect makes a decent man." The video went viral, and women around the world found their new hero.

So how did a bartender from the Bronx become one of America's, nay, the world's most important political figures? It's simple, really: she knew exactly what her constituents needed. She knew because she was one of them.

"I am experienced enough to do this. I am knowledgeable enough to do this. I am prepared enough to do this. I am mature enough to do this. I am brave enough to do this."

Alexandria Ocasio-Cortez

Lentil Salad with Mango and Avocado

YIELD: 4–6 SERVINGS

Community support can look like a lot of things, whether it involves pleasantries in the hallway, a listening ear in the elevator, or a nutritious meal delivered to a neighbor. Most of us are not in a position to pack our notebook, red lipstick, and tools for change all the way over to the Capitol like AOC can, but we CAN use food as a tether to connect us with the communities we find ourselves in. Think Bronx block party!

For this recipe, we brought together the sustaining force of black lentils and unleashed a whole lot of bright, vibrant flavors on top. Here you'll find sweet mango, creamy avocado, peppery greens, and pickled red chilies (for an important spicy layer and that signature red touch). This dish is sharable, approachable, and perfect for nearly any occasion.

Now go clink glasses with neighbors, share conversations over tasty legumes, and dream big about what your community really could be if you dared to change it. AOC would be proud!

RECIPE

1 cup beluga lentils

Zest and juice of 1 lime

½ medium red onion, thinly sliced

¼ cup champagne vinegar (see note for vinegar alternatives)

1 tablespoon Dijon mustard

1 teaspoon honey

1 teaspoon sea salt

Freshly cracked pepper to taste

6 tablespoons olive oil

½ cup chopped fresh cilantro, parsley, and/or basil

A couple good handfuls of arugula or other peppery green of choice

1 mango, peeled and thinly sliced

1 avocado, peeled and thinly sliced
Pickled chilies, optional but highly recommended (recipe on page 47)

- Bring 3 cups of salted water to a boil. Add the lentils, and cook for 20 to 25 minutes. They should be tender with a slight bite in the middle and should not fall apart. Drain well, and cool in a bowl.

- Combine the lime juice and zest in a small bowl and add the sliced onions, toss to coat, and let stand for at least 10 minutes.

- Make the vinaigrette in a medium bowl. Whisk together the vinegar, Dijon mustard, honey, salt, and pepper together. Slowly drizzle in the olive oil while whisking until emulsified. Check for flavor balance.

- Add the lentils and chopped herbs to the bowl of vinaigrette and fold together. Allow the mixture to sit for a few minutes to marry.

- Fold in the pickled onions (along with their juices) and arugula. Top with slices of mango, avocado, and pickled chilies before serving.

Note: *Beluga lentils are worth seeking out. Not only are they a striking color and perfectly beadlike in shape, but they don't require any presoaking (YAY!), so you can literally whip up this salad in any season for any occasion and in just thirty minutes! As for the vinegar, we call for champagne vinegar, which is a slightly sweet white wine vinegar, perfect for salad dressings. If this is hard to find, you can use another red or white wine vinegar and add an extra tablespoon of honey to the dressing.*

RECIPE PAIRING IDEA

Bring this salad to a community feast near you! Alongside Junko Tabei's Bold Peanutty Shrimp (page 118) and a pitcher of Rupi Kaur's Summer Shrub (page 208), you're looking at a meal that really brings people together.

The Question at the Table

In what ways can you work to build up your community?
Think small or big—it all counts!

IRENA SENDLER

POLAND, 1910–2008

> "You see a man drowning, you must try
> to save him even if you cannot swim."

Picture it as though it were a scene from a movie, because if anything deserves a moment captured on film, it is this...

A woman stands at the foot of an apple tree, shovel in hand. She has just buried the last jar containing the identities of thousands of Jewish children. Under her feet lie any hope for those children to be reunited with their families.

The woman's name is Irena Sendler, and she was a Polish nurse and social worker during World War II. As head of the children's division of the underground resistance organization Żegota (Polish Council to Aid Jews), she helped smuggle approximately twenty-five hundred Jewish children out of the Warsaw ghetto, providing them with false identities in non-Jewish families. Suspected of involvement with the Polish underground, in 1943, Irena was arrested, tortured, and imprisoned by the Gestapo.

She revealed nothing of her work—not one location of the saved children. She held on to the hope that the children would someday reunite with their families. Though nothing could obscure the beauty of her selfless act, this part of Irena's story does not end well. The majority of those children's parents and grandparents, aunts and uncles would perish in the death camps and ovens of the Holocaust.

Regardless—for there must always be a *regardless*, even in such dark times (maybe especially in such dark times)—Irena's efforts saved thousands of young lives, sparing them from the evils of the Holocaust. She is justly remembered by Israel and Poland, among others, for the overwhelming love that shone through Europe's darkest time.

Garlicky Breadcrumbs with Broccoli and Feta

YIELD: 4–6 SERVINGS

Remember Hansel and Gretel? Brother and sister leave home with a loaf of stale bread, leaving breadcrumbs in their wake as they venture deeper into the dark forest. Breadcrumbs alone led them home, away from danger.

Irena Sendler left similar clues behind for the twenty-five hundred lives she saved. She buried those crumbs under a tree, hoping to unearth them and reunite torn families. Fate had other plans.

We celebrate her effort nonetheless. Yes, this recipe has broccoli, pickled chili peppers, and feta cheese, but let's be honest—it's about the breadcrumbs. Fried in garlicky butter until golden brown, they are the reason for this dish's existence.

This recipe is a great reason to stop throwing away those leftover hunks of bread. Tear them up by hand and pulse them in a food processor—but not too much. Irregularity is what gives these breadcrumbs their allure. We store ours in the freezer and fry them up a handful at a time for dishes throughout the week.

RECIPE

4 tablespoons olive oil, divided

1 tablespoon unsalted butter

2 medium cloves fresh garlic, peeled and thinly sliced

1 cup fresh breadcrumbs (see above)

1 teaspoon sea salt, divided

1 pound broccoli, broken into florets

Freshly cracked black pepper

½ cup crumbled feta cheese
Pickled chilies (recipe below)

- Heat a 10-inch pan, preferably with a fitted lid, over medium heat. Add 2 tablespoons of the olive oil and the butter, followed by the sliced garlic. Watch it sizzle, and just before it begins to turn golden, add the breadcrumbs. Constantly move the mixture around in the hot pan until it takes on a nutty aroma and a deep golden color. Add a dash of olive oil or a small knob of butter to moisten the mixture if it looks too dry. Season with ½ teaspoon of the salt, empty the contents of the pan into a bowl, and set aside. Give the pan a quick wipe with a towel to remove excess crumbs.

- Reheat the pan over medium heat. Add ¼ cup water and the broccoli florets. Cover with a fitted lid, lower the heat, and steam for 6 to 8 minutes. Check for doneness by piercing the stems of the largest florets with the tip of a knife. It should enter with only a little resistance. Take off the lid for the last minute to allow the last of the water to evaporate.

- Add the remaining 2 tablespoons of olive oil, the remaining salt, and the freshly cracked black pepper, and turn the heat up to high. Allow some of the broccoli to brown on the bottom. Give the pan a shake once or twice. Pour the broccoli out into a low bowl. Sprinkle the cup of toasted breadcrumbs over the broccoli, and top with crumbled feta and pickled chilies, as desired.

QUICK PICKLED CHILIES

¼ cup white vinegar

2 teaspoons sugar

2 teaspoons sea salt

6 medium-hot red chili peppers (like Fresno chilies), sliced into thin rings

- Combine the vinegar, sugar, and salt with ½ cup water in a sealable jar, and mix or shake until the sugar and salt have dissolved slightly. Add the chilies, seal the lid, and put in the fridge.

NOTE: *The chilies can be used after just one day, but they are really spectacular after a whole week and beyond.*

RECIPE PAIRING IDEA

This dish is loaded with flavor diversity—it's crunchy, tender, salty, spicy, tangy, and creamy all at once! So basically, it's a brilliant side dish for anything you are cooking up. But we can suggest that pairing it with Junko Tabei's Bold Peanutty Shrimp (page 118) or maybe even with Zitkala-Sa's Skillet Maize with Spicy Cherry Tomato Salsa (page 62) won't leave you disappointed in the flavor or company department.

The Question at the Table

If you could be reunited with one of your deceased relatives
for one day, who would it be, and why?

OPRAH WINFREY

USA, 1954–

> "Self-esteem comes from being able to define the world in your own terms and refusing to abide by the judgments of others."

Born into poverty to a teenage single mother in rural Mississippi, Oprah Winfrey lived her early years experiencing acute abuse and oppression in inner-city Milwaukee. She was abused, molested, and sexually assaulted. She was impregnated at fourteen and gave birth to a premature son, who died soon after birth.

People used to call scenarios like this "humble beginnings," glossing over the pain and injustice women endured while also minimizing their strength.

There's no minimizing Oprah though. Go ahead and try—she's got no time for naysayers and never has. By nineteen, she was already cohosting the evening news in Tennessee. In a short time, she was in the daytime slot. Not long after that, she took a Chicago talk show from third to first place before starting her own production company. At thirty-two, she was only getting started.

Oprah made her acting debut in 1985 in *The Color Purple*. As the character Sofia, a fiercely courageous and independent mother, Oprah's own voice and convictions boomed from the screen, reverberating in the hearts of audiences around the world. The role won her a nomination for an Academy Award, proving she was not only a natural in front of live television audiences, but a talent to be reckoned with on the big screen.

With that being said, Oprah still remains best known for her talk show, *The Oprah Winfrey Show* (1986–2011), the highest-rated television program of its kind in history. She used this platform to inspire, uplift, and listen to the stories of others and their unique experiences. The show was groundbreaking for its time and continues to be relevant today.

Oprah eventually became the wealthiest Black American of the twentieth century, called not only the greatest Black philanthropist in American history but also the most influential woman in the world. In 2013, President Barack Obama awarded her the Presidential Medal of Freedom. And in further recognition, she has received honorary doctorate degrees from Duke and Harvard.

We've honestly barely touched the surface of Oprah's profound accomplishments, but what better way to wrap this up than with a slice of her own sound advice?

"Breathe. Let go. And remind yourself that this very moment is the only one you know you have for sure."

Oprah Winfrey

Purple Potato Salad with Fried Capers

YIELD: 4–6 SERVINGS

A huge task, choosing just one of Oprah's accomplishments to highlight in a recipe. Because she's a lover of good food and calls Santa Barbara, California, home, we wanted to create a dish that reminds us of that beautiful coastal city but also spoke up bright and strong.

Maybe hitting it a bit on the nose with *The Color Purple*, we took that regal color, added lots of fresh green herbs, a tangy mustard and wine-based vinaigrette, and topped it with fried caper blossoms.

It's a dish that makes a statement and refuses to be ordinary—much like Oprah herself.

RECIPE

2 pounds small purple potatoes

2 tablespoons good dry white wine

2 tablespoons chicken stock (or vegetable stock)

3 tablespoons white balsamic vinegar

2 teaspoons Dijon mustard

1 teaspoon sea salt, divided

¾ teaspoon freshly cracked black pepper, divided

¾ cup olive oil, divided

¼ cup capers, drained and dried on a towel

¼ cup minced green onions (white and green parts)

2 tablespoons finely chopped fresh dill

2 tablespoons finely chopped flat-leaf parsley

2 tablespoons julienned fresh basil leaves

Oprah Winfrey

- Drop the potatoes into a large pot of boiling salted water and cook for 20 to 30 minutes (depending on the size), until they are just cooked through. You can check for doneness by piercing the potatoes with the sharp tip of a paring knife—there should be no resistance. Drain in a colander, and place a towel over the potatoes to allow them to steam for 10 more minutes.

- Cut the potatoes into ½-inch slices, and place in a medium bowl. Toss gently with the wine and chicken stock. Allow the liquids to soak into the warm potatoes before proceeding.

- Combine the vinegar, mustard, ½ teaspoon salt, and ¼ teaspoon pepper, and slowly whisk in ½ cup of olive oil to make an emulsion.

- Heat the remaining olive oil in a small skillet. When the oil is "dancing" (when you see movement from heat), add the dry capers. Fry for a minute or two, shaking the pan slightly to move the capers in the hot oil. Look for the blossoms (capers are a flower!) to unwrap slightly and the edges to begin to brown. Watch out for popping! Take them out with a slotted spoon, and drain on a paper towel. Sprinkle with ¼ teaspoon salt.

- Add the vinaigrette to the potatoes, followed by the green onions, dill, parsley, basil, and remaining salt and pepper. Toss, and top with fried capers. Serve at room temperature.

RECIPE PAIRING IDEA

This recipe can cozy up well on your picnic blanket at the beach or on your favorite grassy bluff. May we suggest you pack up Greta Thunberg's Cashew Chipotle Dip (page 34) with crunchy things to drag through it and Jane Goodall's Palm Sugar Banana Bread (page 178) as well. Now that is really the ultimate picnic company!

The Question at the Table

What are you the queen or king of? Or what would those who know you best say you are the queen or king of?

Oprah Winfrey

RUTH BADER GINSBURG

USA, 1933–2020

"My mother told me to be a lady. And for her, that meant be your own person, be independent."

It's safe to say this at least: rarely do the lives of deceased rappers and Supreme Court justices intersect as amusingly as in the case of the Notorious RBG. In 2013, an NYU grad student gave then-eighty-year-old Ruth Bader Ginsburg the moniker in celebration of her impassioned, principled dissents—and, like the late Notorious B.I.G., an absolute refusal to compromise one's vision.

Following a legal career advocating for women's rights and gender equality, RBG took the oath of office for the Supreme Court, becoming the second woman to hold the position. For three years, she was the *only woman* on the bench. Rather than be cowed by being a minority, RBG became even more forceful in her dissents.

Until the 2018 term, in fact, RBG had not missed a single day of oral arguments—no, not even when she underwent chemotherapy for pancreatic cancer, after surgery for colon cancer, or the day following her husband's passing in 2010.

The country took notice, and from the early 2010s to her passing in 2020, she became more than just one of nine Supreme Court justices. She became a figure we depended on for our sense of security. We relied upon her strength to defend us, to keep safe the principles for which we stand.

Long live those principles. Long live the legacy of RBG.

Smashed Potatoes with Crème Fraîche and Caviar

YIELD: 4–6 SERVINGS

Don't think you deserve something this delicious? Take a lesson from RBG: you *do* deserve it, because you put in the work and you've got taste.

Lemme break it down for you.

During personal training sessions, the eighty-six-year-old RBG used to regularly do twenty push-ups, all while listening to classical music. *You read that right*.

With roots in NYC and Russian-Jewish tradition, it's no surprise RBG had a dope sense of deli flavor. She sometimes ordered in smoked salmon and caviar from one of her favorites, a deli on the Lower East Side by the name of Russ & Daughters.

(Not Russ & *Sons*, y'all! Even when procuring her favorite snacks, RBG made her position *known*.)

We took some cues for sure, creating a dish that is a workout, a flavor feast, *and* a statement all at once. By smashing a simple potato—*note: it is extremely important you do this while imagining smashing the patriarchy as a whole*—a brand new meal is created. Fried in garlic and a spoonful of butter, topped with caviar, crème fraîche, and bright herbs, there's nothing you won't love about this dish.

(Of course, should you really want to do RBG proud, go ahead and splurge: fly in some of that caviar from Russ & Daughters!)

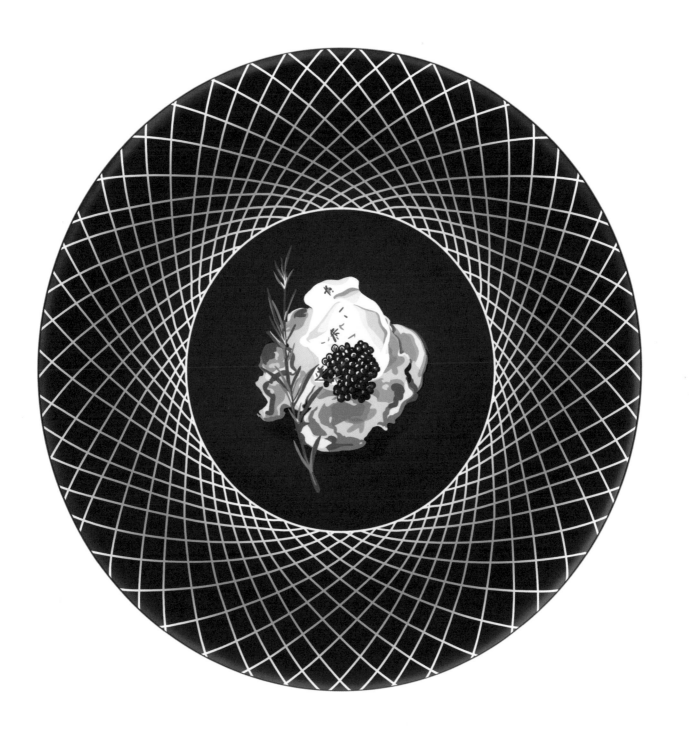

RECIPE

1 ¼ pounds small potatoes (1 to 2 inches, about the size
    of a golf ball)
Sea salt
¼ cup chicken fat or olive oil
Freshly cracked black pepper
3 tablespoons unsalted butter, divided
½ small yellow onion, thinly sliced into rings
4 medium cloves fresh garlic, thinly sliced
4 sprigs thyme
½ teaspoon crushed red pepper flakes
¼ cup chopped fresh flat-leaf parsley
¾ cup crème fraîche
2 to 4 ounces caviar (in true RBG fashion, but completely optional)
Flaky salt to finish

- Bring 2 inches of water to a boil in a large, heavy-bottomed pot fitted with a steamer basket. Add the potatoes, and season with salt. Cover and steam until the potatoes are cooked through, 8 to 10 minutes. (Check one of the smaller ones after 8 minutes to see how tender it is; you should be able to insert a fork into it easily.) If you don't have a steamer basket, boil them in a large pot of salted water until tender, 10 to 15 minutes.

- Remove the potatoes from the steamer, and let them cool slightly. Use the bottom of a bowl or cup, or the palm of your hand to smash the potatoes until they're just crushed to expose the inside, but not so much that they fall apart. You're going for maximum crispy surface area here.

- Heat the chicken fat (or olive oil) in a large, heavy-bottomed skillet over medium-high heat. Add the potatoes in a single layer (work in batches if you need to), and season with salt and black pepper. Cook for about 4 to 5 minutes until very browned and crispy. Flip over, add ½ tablespoon butter to the pan, and cook for another 4 to 5 minutes.

- Remove potatoes with a slotted spoon or spatula, and transfer to a serving bowl or platter. Add the rest of the butter to the skillet, and let it melt and foam. Add the onion rings, garlic, and thyme in a single layer, and season with salt and black pepper. Cook, swirling skillet occasionally until the onions have turned golden brown and started to crisp, 3 to 5 minutes.

Ruth Bader Ginsburg

- Remove the skillet from the heat, and add red pepper flakes, swirling the skillet a few times to combine. Pour the onions, garlic, thyme, and any butter in the skillet over the potatoes, and top with flaky salt, parsley, dollops of crème fraîche. and if the spirit of RBG compels you (as we're sure she would!), spoonfuls of caviar atop each potato.

RECIPE PAIRING IDEA

What could you possibly serve with such sophisticated potatoes? May we suggest inviting Buffy Sainte-Marie's Green Goddess Salad (page 2) and Chimamanda Ngozi Adichie's Salted Dark Chocolate Raspberry Tart (page 140)? Talk about a dream dinner party: RBG, BSM, and CNA! Be still, our hearts!

The Question at the Table

What are you notorious for?

ZITKALA-SA

USA, 1876–1938

> "I seem to be in a spiritual unrest. I hate this eternal tug of war between being wild or becoming civilized. I am what I am. I owe no apologies to God or men."

Among the Sioux of South Dakota in the late 1800s, short hair was only worn by mourners or cowards. Upon entering a missionary-run boarding school, however, a Sioux child's hair was immediately cut—the first step in erasing that child's cultural identity and replacing it with white American identity.

Zitkala-Sa (Red Bird) of the Sioux Tribe was only eight years old in 1884 when Quaker missionaries persuaded her to leave the Yankton Sioux reservation to attend a boarding school in Indiana. She was given the new name of Gertrude Simmons, yet another step in the process of imperfect assimilation.

As an older woman—when she was well known as a writer, translator, and editor as well as musician and activist—she spoke often about the joy of learning to read and write, of learning to play the violin, but she also expressed the deep grief of losing her heritage. She was one of the first Indigenous American women to publish traditional stories derived from the oral tradition. She wrote several works chronicling her struggles with cultural identity, and she published several exposés about the trauma Indigenous children experienced in boarding schools.

In 1913, Zitkala-Sa wrote the first Indigenous American opera, *The Sun Dance Opera*. It was a collaboration with white composer William Hanson, inspired by a sacred ceremony of spiritual healing, a dance of personal devotion and sacrifice outlawed by the U.S. government. Opera was a calculated choice, as it mirrored her people's oral storytelling and tapped into American high society.

The later years of her life were dedicated to activism for the land's true people. "There is no doubt I have in the direction I wish to go—to spend my energies working for the Indian race." Her work contributed to the passing of the Indian Citizenship Act of 1924. She knew there were two worlds that Indigenous people had to straddle and that they must have power in both. "The answers to Indian issues lay in Indian people themselves."

The fight to reclaim sacred land, the search for missing native women, and the right of Indigenous voices to be heard are still ongoing today. The voice of Zitkala-Sa rises from her mother earth, from the very soil under our feet, weaving words between the worlds of what was native land and is now the United States.

SAVORY

Skillet Maize with Spicy Cherry Tomato Salsa

YIELD: 4–6 SERVINGS

Maize was arguably the most important staple food grown by Indigenous Americans. It's long been a symbol of sustenance—the simple image of a stalk of corn, the staff of life—but it was also an important ritualistic item for many tribes. Maize is considered a gift from the Great Spirit, with a role both as food and ceremonial object. Ground maize (cornmeal) is considered sacred and used to bless and nurture people and objects, sort of the way certain Christian groups use holy water.

We pay homage to this sacred grain here. After all, so many of us have our own connection to the plant. Maybe we ran through cornfields in late summer, stumbled around trying to find our way out of a corn maze, shucked corn by the lakeside, or rolled bright yellow ears of corn over cold sticks of salted butter. All who claim America as their home have a relationship with the giant stalks that rise toward the sun.

Zitkala-Sa

"We must stand straight and firm like an arrow, pointing in the direction of our dreams," Zitkala-Sa said.

Families in the heart of the Midwest make corn casserole in the summer months. It's a savory dish that errs substantially on the sweet side, made with a box of Jiffy corn muffin mix and canned corn, bound together with eggs and sour cream, and baked in your best Pyrex rectangle.

We've created our own version, filled with fresh corn and more savory than sweet from parmesan, green onions, and plenty of cracked black pepper. Made into a full meal with an accessory salsa of halved cherry tomatoes, fresh cilantro, and spicy green chilies, it's a dish that is both wild and civilized.

Like a ceremony of remembrance, may you nourish your loved ones with the legacy of Zitkala-Sa and this dish of sacred maize.

RECIPE

4 tablespoons unsalted butter, divided

2 green onions, white and light green parts, thinly sliced

1 jalapeño pepper, half seeded and thinly sliced, other half reserved for salsa

1 teaspoon sea salt, plus two pinches, divided

4 cups fresh corn, cut off the cob (about 4 medium cobs)

1 clove fresh garlic, finely chopped

½ teaspoon ground cumin

Freshly cracked black pepper to taste

1 ½ cups heavy cream

2 eggs

6 tablespoons cornmeal

2 tablespoons brown sugar

1 ½ teaspoons baking powder

½ cup freshly grated parmesan, Manchego, or pecorino cheese

- Preheat the oven to 350°F, and grease a 9-by-9-inch baking dish with 2 tablespoons of butter.

- Set a medium skillet over medium heat, and melt the remaining butter. Add the green onions, sliced jalapeño, and a pinch of salt. Sauté for 5 minutes, stirring occasionally, until soft. Add the corn kernels and cook, stirring often, for another 5 minutes. Turn off the heat.

- Add the garlic, cumin, another pinch of salt, and cracked pepper to taste. Let cool while you tend to the rest of the recipe.

- Combine the cream, eggs, and 1 teaspoon of salt in a bowl. Whisk with a fork until smooth.

- Combine the cornmeal, brown sugar, baking powder, and cheese in a large bowl. Stir with a spoon or rubber spatula until combined. Add the corn mixture, followed by the liquid mixture, and stir. Pour into the prepared baking dish.

- Bake for 35 to 45 minutes until the skillet maize has puffed up and is deeply browned along the edges and browning on top. Cool for a few minutes before serving. Cut or spoon out portions, and serve with a side of Spicy Cherry Tomato Salsa.

SPICY CHERRY TOMATO SALSA

1 pint fresh cherry tomatoes, halved
¼ cup chopped cilantro
¼ cup red onion, sliced into ¼-by-1-inch sticks
1 tablespoon olive oil
Reserved jalapeño pepper, seeded and finely minced
Zest and juice of half a lime
Flaky salt and freshly cracked black pepper to taste

- Combine all the ingredients in a medium bowl. Stir and taste for balance.

RECIPE PAIRING IDEA

This dish would pair brilliantly with Frida Kahlo's Self-Illustrated Tortilla Soup (page 82) or alongside Alexandria Ocasio-Cortez's Lentil Salad with Mango and Avocado (page 40).

SAVORY

The Question at the Table

When have you felt torn between two roles or contradictory parts of yourself?

MEGAN RAPINOE

USA, 1985–

"Sometimes it's worth risking it all for a dream only you can see."

If you had to name only one head of hair that best sums up *leader*, whose head of hair would it be?

We think Megan Rapinoe is the obvious answer. I mean, c'mon. You can't see the pink locks of the U.S. Women's National Soccer Team's former captain without saying *whoa* under your breath. And if you've seen her play or speak out against racial and gender injustice, you've seen skill, conviction, and humility. Few figures in sports today can claim to have stood so tall for issues so important.

Rattling the cage for equality and recognition in women's sports for years, Megan represents her teammates demanding equality in soccer. In 2019, she and twenty-seven teammates from the U.S. Women's National Soccer Team filed a lawsuit against the U.S. Soccer Federation, accusing it of gender discrimination.

Megan, one of the oldest players in the league as well as its most recognizable voice in social justice spaces, has been outspoken about the lawsuit. "This has always been a team fight, and it dates back generations," she said, arguing that she and her teammates have been subjected to "institutionalized gender discrimination"—smaller paychecks, worse travel accommodations, and subpar field conditions compared to their male counterparts. Since the onset of the U.S. Women's Soccer lawsuit, women across the globe are demanding equal pay and rights as well.

On and off the field, Megan leans into the role as leader and collaborator, refusing sole acknowledgment for her team's accomplishments—very likely an outgrowth of her own upbringing in an open-minded household where roles were not determined by gender. She summed up her relationship to her family when she said, "They are in me, and I am in them." While her natural talent and hard-fought skill are apparent, she attributes much of her success to this cooperative outlook: for years, she encouraged others to succeed at the same time as she strived for greatness.

None of which is to downplay Megan's actual, y'know, athletic skill. *Goal* comes to mind, just as it does with Alex Morgan or Hayley Wickenheiser. In fact, go search "Megan Rapinoe's greatest goals."

We'll wait, because this is important.

Wow, right? You try that. No, really—put your shoes on and practice before this meal! It's what Megan would do. Just don't hurt yourself!

The truth is, Megan's no different from us, really, even with that fly hair. As we journey through life, we gather our own support: our tribe, our village. Those who will share the field with us and fight for our success as we fight for theirs.

We'd encourage you to be more like Megan, but we know what she'd say in response:

Be more like *the team*.

A Winning Breakfast Sandwich

YIELD: 2 SANDWICHES

Food as fuel is something Megan Rapinoe knows well. Considering the amount of nutrients she needs to energize her body, food is the main thing keeping her fired up, but she also maintains a hard line between what's good *for her*, and what's actually *goooooooood*. For example, she once said, "I avoid almost all dairy...except when it's an artisanal cheese platter. Then I get fully involved."

Fully. Involved. Oh, we hear you there, Megan. We're basically plant-based with a side of bacon. It's totally a thing.

Still, starting the day with excellent nutrition is important for athletes. Alongside her multiple cups of good coffee in the morning, Megan likes to make a couple of fried eggs topped with sautéed onions and spinach, nestled in an English muffin.

We dream of sharing that meal with Megan, her excellent hair all mussed as she sits down to eat. We'd be distracted, obviously—worried about being cool enough to *hang*, y'know?—but we'd also understand how much work we put into making the right meal for her, a breakfast sandwich not unlike her own but with an extra bit of flair.

This triumph is loaded with spinach, smashed avocado, and savory fried eggs, all stuffed between Gruyère-fried bread. It's like making a quick goal at the artisanal cheese platter!

RECIPE

¼ cup whole milk yogurt or vegan yogurt

1 clove fresh garlic

Sea salt and freshly cracked black pepper

Pinch of crushed red pepper flakes

4 tablespoons olive oil

4 slices good bread (see note below), about ¾-inch thick

½ cup Gruyère or sharp cheddar, coarsely grated

2 large eggs
1 ripe avocado, halved and smashed
2 handfuls fresh spinach, arugula, or other dark leafy green

- Place the yogurt in a small bowl, and finely grate the garlic clove on top. Season with a pinch of salt, plenty of cracked black pepper, and red pepper flakes. Stir well and set aside.

- Heat a medium nonstick skillet over medium heat, and add 1 tablespoon olive oil. Fry the slices of bread, adding more oil as necessary to give the slices a nice golden color on each side. When the fried bread is almost finished, lift the slices up one by one and sprinkle about 2 tablespoons of the grated Gruyère directly on the pan. Press the bread slices down onto the sizzling cheese for about 30 seconds. Use a spatula to take the bread out of the pan, and set aside while you fry the eggs in the pan with more oil, cooking as desired. Now it's time to assemble your sandwich. Top the cheese-fried bread with a spoonful of garlicky yogurt, a dollop of smashed avocado, spinach leaves, the fried egg, and a pinch more salt and pepper.

- Top the sandwich with the other slice of cheese-fried bread, and enjoy!

NOTE: *Bread choice is entirely up to you, depending on what you can get your hands on. We love a good rustic loaf, French boule, or sourdough bread—something with a good crunchy crust. Of course, you can be like Megan and stick to the English muffin, and we won't blame you: no one can deny that an English muffin makes a great breakfast sandwich! The only type of bread we'd specifically avoid is presliced sandwich bread. Cheese choices are flexible as well: aged parmesan or sharp English cheddar are great substitutes for Gruyère. Something sharp and aged is best all around.*

RECIPE PAIRING IDEA

Add teammate Judy Chicago with her Ginger Brûléed Grapefruit (page 154) or Amelia Earhart's Rich Hot Chocolate (page 202) for a real winning breakfast.

The Question at the Table

How would you describe your relationship to taking on leadership roles?

MARSHA P. JOHNSON

USA, 1945–1992

"I was no one, nobody, from Nowheresville until I became a drag queen. That's what made me in New York, that's what made me in New Jersey, that's what made me in the world."

You can't really know what it's like to be another person, but sometimes you try. As a friend. As an ally.

It's the 1960s. You've just graduated from high school. You're Black and gay and transgender. You take your possessions, which amount to a bag of clothes and fifteen dollars in cash, and move to Manhattan, New York—one of the most tolerant places for LGBTQ+ people you can find. Tolerant, but nowhere near perfect. Police regularly harass those who don't conform to rigid gender roles.

Someone like Marsha P. Johnson, who'd begun wearing dresses at the age of five, can't acquire or keep a job. She is frequently homeless, surviving through prostitution.

Now that you've imagined the hardship, turn your mind to love and joy: known for her cheerful personality and ostentatious homemade outfits, complete with holiday tinsel in her wigs, Marsha became one of the most prominent figures in the New York LGBTQ+ community.

She was open and giving, earning the nickname "Saint Marsha." She and trans activist and friend Sylvia Rivera formed Street Transvestite Action Revolutionaries (STAR), turning a donated apartment into a shelter for homeless trans people.

Now, imagine courage. Though the accounts vary, it's clear that in 1969, Marsha became one of the pivotal figures in the Stonewall Riots. Perhaps, as many have claimed, she started the riots by throwing a shot glass into a mirror. This "shot glass heard round the world" is celebrated by the LGBTQ+ community to this day—hallowed as a symbol of resistance.

Throughout the 1970s, '80s, and '90s, Marsha continued resisting—in big ways, helping individuals suffering from AIDS, and in small ways, insisting on her own dignity and privacy. That "P" in her name? It stands for "Pay it no mind," the response she gave to people confused by her gender designation.

In July 1992, Marsha's body was pulled from the Hudson River. Police ruled it a suicide without conducting an investigation. Her friends insisted otherwise, and through their advocacy, the case was reopened in 2012. It remains an open case.

In life, Marsha celebrated humanity. In death, she reminds us to keep fighting for justice.

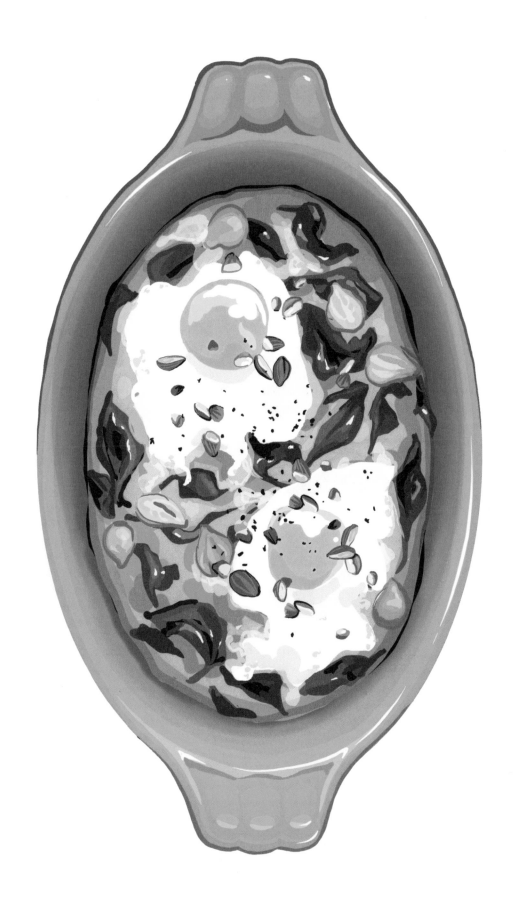

Golden Baked Eggs

YIELD: 2–4 SERVINGS

Vibrant eggs floating on seasoned cream, loaded with spinach and golden tomatoes—the dish we created for Marsha is perhaps the most striking in the book, paying homage to the joy she took in her style, the way she turned heads with each showstopping look. It also echoes some of our favorite egg dishes from other countries: North African shakshuka, English coddled eggs, the Moroccan Berber omelet, or Italy's *uova in purgatorio* (eggs in purgatory).

Pay that last bit no mind though. This dish isn't stuck in purgatory, somewhere between heaven and hell. Our Golden Baked Eggs ascend on the taste buds like a saint rising to the clouds.

No need to top your wig with tinsel this holiday season. Just put out your prettiest dish with these Golden Baked Eggs, and give cheers to Saint Marsha!

RECIPE

3 tablespoons unsalted butter, divided

1 medium shallot, thinly sliced

1 small clove fresh garlic, grated

¼ teaspoon ground turmeric

Sea salt and freshly cracked black pepper to taste

Pinch of crushed red pepper flakes

6 to 8 golden cherry tomatoes, halved lengthwise, divided

1 cup packed fresh baby spinach

¾ cup heavy cream

4 eggs

¼ cup smoked almonds, roughly chopped

Chopped chives (optional)

Crusty bread

Marsha P. Johnson

- Set a rack in the center of the oven, and preheat to 425°F.

- Butter an 8-inch ovenproof dish with 1 tablespoon of the butter, and set aside.

- Melt the remaining butter in a medium pan over medium-high heat. Add the shallot and garlic, and cook for just a minute or so for the shallot to begin to soften and become translucent, stirring often. Add the ground turmeric, salt, pepper, red pepper flakes, and half of the halved cherry tomatoes. Stir and cook down for another minute before turning off the heat.

- Pour the seasoned shallot mixture into the prepared oven dish, and spread out evenly. Scatter the baby spinach leaves evenly over the top. Pour the cream over all the colorful vegetables, and then crack the four eggs on top of that. Season with another pinch of salt and pepper to continue to layer the flavors.

- Bake the egg dish in the center of the oven for 6 minutes (1 minute longer for firmer egg yolks), until the egg yolks wiggle slightly when you shake the pan but the whites are no longer translucent. Turn the top broiler on, and leave the eggs in for one more minute to welcome some caramelization to the cream.

- Top with a scatter of smoked almonds and chopped chives, and serve with good crusty bread.

NOTE: *For all you dairy-free folks out there, feel free to switch tomato sauce for the cream and olive oil for the butter!*

SAVORY

RECIPE PAIRING IDEA

If you plan on serving this dish for brunch, consider inviting Judy Chicago and her Ginger Brûléed Grapefruit (page 154) and Aretha Franklin's Peaches and Biscuits (page 158) to the table as well for a truly vibrant spread.

The Question at the Table

When was a time that you felt different but extremely proud to be?

FRIDA KAHLO

MEXICO, 1907–1954

> "They thought I was a surrealist,
> but I wasn't. I never painted dreams.
> I painted my own reality."

Wouldn't you agree that fighting polio, suffering a horrific auto accident, undergoing more than thirty surgeries, and having a miscarriage kinda seem like enough for one life?

Nope. Meet Frida Kahlo.

Physical limitations shaped her life from an early age. At six years old, she contracted polio, leaving her bedridden for nine months. In spite of her remaining limp, her father encouraged her to lean into physical activity. And that is what she did. Standing out among the other girls of her time, she swam, she wrestled, and she played soccer. She learned early on to find healing by challenging her strength. Unfortunately, physical suffering and trauma continued to haunt her, testing that strength again and again.

But, and this is a BIG but, Frida was able to channel her pain into beauty through a paintbrush and a blank canvas. Much of her work as an artist was done while lying down in a hospital bed during her many stages of recovery.

She painted with a freedom generations of silenced women could only dream about, deviating from the traditional depiction of women, choosing instead to express the rawness of female experiences and challenges. During the early 1900s, the gritty realities faced by women were kept private, out of sight. What happened to women behind hospital, bedroom, and bathroom doors was rarely seen, treated as if it never happened at all. But nothing stopped Frida. She faced what was considered shameful and taboo head on, depicting pregnancies, miscarriages, menstruation, breastfeeding, birth, infertility, and sexual organs throughout her paintings. What she created was groundbreaking, shedding a bright light onto the shared experience of womankind.

Frida also defied gender stereotypes. She smoked, boxed, and won tequila matches against men. Some days, she dressed like a man in a suit without altering her natural unibrow or faint mustache. Other days, she layered beautiful textiles over long skirts paired with red lipstick and flowers braided in her hair. Through the intertwining of these identities, she helped to weave the brilliant fabrics of gender fluidity for all of us to wear. Nothing stopped Frida. Be like Frida—which of course means *Be fearlessly yourself.*

Frida Kahlo

Self-Illustrated Tortilla Soup

YIELD: 4–6 SERVINGS

Frida's uniqueness lay in the way she depicted herself in her paintings. She followed her heart and mind to express herself in a way that did not fit the acceptable norms of the time.

Cooking, like painting, is an act of self-expression. This soup offers space for interpretation and freedom to innovate as well: the base is a blank canvas to draw flavor upon. Fill tiny bowls with ingredients, like palettes of color across your table, and allow each person to compose their dish as they feel. Remember Frida, who was always fiercely *herself*, as you share this soup. *Buen provecho!*

RECIPE

6 cups chicken stock

3 boneless, skinless chicken breasts

Neutral oil for frying

2 small to medium yellow onions, chopped

4 tomatoes, chopped, or 1 (14-ounce) can chopped tomatoes

1 carrot, grated

2 cloves fresh garlic, chopped

Sea salt to taste

10 small corn tortillas, julienned into matchsticks

1 teaspoon dried oregano

1 jalapeño pepper, seeded and finely chopped

Freshly cracked black pepper to taste

Squeeze of lime

1 bunch cilantro, chopped

1 small red onion, finely chopped or thinly sliced

Sour cream

Avocado, chopped or thinly sliced

3–4 radishes, thinly sliced

Queso fresco, cheddar cheese, or another sharp favorite
    cheese, crumbled, shaved, or grated
6 lime wedges

- Heat the chicken stock in a medium-sized pot, add the chicken breasts, and simmer until cooked through, about 10 minutes. Feel free to check color and doneness by cutting one breast open. Remove the chicken breasts from the stock, and set aside to cool on a separate plate. Once cool enough to handle, shred the chicken with your fingers into strips. Set the stock aside.

- Heat 2 tablespoons of oil in a large pot, and add the onions. Cook until translucent, and add tomatoes, carrot, and garlic. Cook over medium-low heat for about 6 minutes.

- Add oil to a separate small-medium pan, and fry the strips of tortillas one handful at a time until golden brown. Toss gently while they cook to ensure even frying. Drain on paper towels, and season with salt.

- Pour the reserved stock into the tomato mixture. Add the oregano and jalapeño (to desired heat level). Stir in 1 cup of the fried tortilla strips, and cook the mixture for 2 minutes on simmer, not a heavy boil. Puree the soup in a blender or with an immersion blender until smooth. Return to the pot, and season with salt and pepper and a squeeze or two of lime.

- Make small bowls for the table each with a different ingredient for topping the soups—remaining tortilla strips, shredded chicken, cilantro, red onion, sour cream, avocado, radishes, cheese, lime wedges, more jalapeño. Get creative!

RECIPE PAIRING IDEA
Consider starting this meal off with corn chips alongside Greta Thunberg's Cashew Chipotle Dip (page 34), and finish off the meal with a bright dessert like Katrín Jakobsdóttir's Wild Blueberry Streusel Cake (page 188).

SAVORY

The Question at the Table

If you could describe your self-portrait in words, what would you say? Please, no negative language here.

INA MAY GASKIN

USA, 1940–

> "If a woman doesn't look like a goddess during labor, then someone isn't treating her right."

Among the many issues confronted by the modern feminist movement, pregnancy and birth generally land somewhere in the "Uh...what?" category. It's as if, despite the prevalence of, y'know, new people, we don't think about the practical politics of pregnancy and birth.

Ina May Gaskin, founder of one of the first out-of-hospital birthing centers in the United States, would like to have some words with you. Why? Because pregnancy and child delivery are among the *biggest* deals for women around the world. Labor is often traumatic, dangerous, and marginalizing. Besides, it's literally the beginning of us all. So let's talk about Ina and her work for a quick sec.

In 1971, Ina and her husband, Stephen—a famed counterculture figure—founded the Farm, an intentional community (commune) based on the themes of nonviolence and ecological awareness, near Summertown, Tennessee. Ina, who had experienced a traumatic delivery during her first pregnancy, founded the Farm Midwifery Center. To date, the center has overseen approximately three thousand births, more than twelve hundred of which Ina has attended.

Ina has changed the conversation about birth in America, reviving old traditions and wisdoms that we, in our push for more technological solutions, had forgotten. She encourages women to be fearless in delivery, to take on the role of hero—warrior goddess and protector!—so that children are born into the world with as little trauma as possible.

For the midwives of the Farm Midwifery Center, this is more than an issue of healthy newborns: it's an issue of a woman's choice, an acknowledgment of her power to do what's right for herself, her family.

Women are, and always have been, the most fearless human beings. We make hard choices, despite the threats against us, over and over again, for the good of our families, our communities. How we welcome our children into this world is arguably the most important of these choices.

Imagine a world where our expertise is validated, our choices respected. Work, like Ina, for *that* world.

Little Bean Soup with Rosemary Salsa Verde

YIELD: 4–6 SERVINGS

Here in Switzerland, where the two of us live, we have this thing we say: *herzige kleine Bohne*. Nearly every adult who sets their gaze on a baby will say this, and it's obvious why. They're all *cute little beans*, aren't they?

We had postpartum mothers in mind when we developed this recipe. Both of us have experienced the delivery spectrum—natural, vaginal births and urgent C-section births. Recovery from either is strongly connected to postpartum nutrition.

We also imagined what Ina would tell a new mother: *Eat. Heal. Celebrate your act of courage and love.* Wrapping your fingers around a warm, nourishing bowl of soup while you gaze at your newborn seems like just the thing a midwife would order for healing and rejuvenation.

Ina May Gaskin

If you would like to make this meal more protein rich, adding a smoked ham hock to the broth works very nicely. The meat can be pulled from the bone after a good hour of cooking slow and low on the stove.

Cheers to little beans and birthing queens!

RECIPE

½ cup olive oil
1 medium onion, finely chopped
1 medium carrot, finely chopped
1 medium stalk celery, finely chopped
2 cloves fresh garlic, finely chopped
1 to 2 teaspoons crushed red pepper flakes, optional
4 cups cannellini beans, canned or made from 1 ½ cups dried beans (preferred), rinsed
4 cups homemade bone broth, vegetable broth, or water
1 (3- to 4-inch) chunk parmesan rind, optional
Sea salt and freshly cracked black pepper
3 cups chopped kale or baby spinach
Juice of 1 lemon
1 ½ cups farro, cooked

- Heat the olive oil in a large pot, and add the onion, carrot, and celery. Cook on medium-low heat, stirring often, for at least 20 minutes to really caramelize the vegetables without making them too brown.

- Add the garlic, red pepper flakes, beans, broth, parmesan chunk, and a good seasoning of salt and pepper. Allow the soup to cook together for at least 30 minutes, best if left on low for over an hour. Make sure it does not boil heavily or stick to the bottom of the pot.

- When you are nearly ready to serve the soup, remove the parmesan rind.

- Use an immersion blender to give the soup 3 to 5 good pulses. You're not trying to make the whole soup velvety and creamy (unless that's your thing, then by all means, go for it!). By breaking up some of the white beans this way, you can create creaminess without losing all the texture from the whole beans.

Ina May Gaskin

- Add the greens and lemon juice, and stir to combine. Test the soup for flavor balance, adding lemon juice for acidity, water if too thick, and salt and pepper if needed.

- Ladle large spoonfuls into soup bowls, add ¼ cup cooked farro to each bowl, and drizzle with Rosemary Salsa Verde.

ROSEMARY SALSA VERDE

½ cup olive oil
¼ cup chopped Italian parsley
1 tablespoon red wine vinegar
1 tablespoon finely chopped fresh rosemary
½ teaspoon flaky salt
1 clove fresh garlic, pounded into puree
Grated zest of 1 lemon
Freshly cracked black pepper
Pinch of crushed red pepper flakes

- Combine all ingredients together in a small bowl. Check for balanced seasoning. Drizzle over warm soup as desired.

RECIPE PAIRING IDEA

Soon-to-be new mothers all enjoy the moment with a belly full of baby, when they begin the nesting phase, filling freezers with soups, stews, and baked goods for the future chaotic days with a new baby in hand. With that in mind, consider inviting Brenda Berkman's Pork Winter Squash Ragù (page 104) and even Jane Goodall's Palm Sugar Banana Bread (page 178) to the list of freezer-friendly goodies.

The Question at the Table

When have you brought life to something meaningful (e.g., a physical being, a passion project, an idea, or a concept)?

SAMPAT PAL DEVI

INDIA, 1960–

> "Village society in India is loaded against women. It refuses to educate them, marries them off too early, barters them for money. Village women need to study and become independent to sort it out themselves."

To those who say violence isn't the answer, meet Sampat Pal Devi—mother, activist, street fighter.

The daughter of a shepherd in Northern India's Uttar Pradesh, Sampat grew up surrounded by men intent on keeping her down. Nonetheless, from a young age, she defined her own way, teaching herself to read, watching the injustice around her with a keen eye.

There were a lot of injustices to see, unfortunately, and she wasn't invulnerable to them. Forced into marriage at the age of twelve, she had five children before turning twenty. Her husband beat her, a common occurrence in Uttar Pradesh.

Rather than back down, Sampat did the extraordinary, fighting back and escaping her husband. When she witnessed another woman being beaten, she took matters into her own hands, returning the next day with a small group of women. They carried sticks. They beat the man in the street.

The Gulabi Gang was born. Dressed in pink saris and armed with bamboo sticks, the Pink Sari Brigade (as they are known in English-speaking countries) boasts over 250,000 members who won't sit on their hands until justice arrives. They refuse to be pushed down, abused, and shoved to the margins. They beat abusers where they find them. They storm police stations, demanding justice for the abused. They stop child marriages and help girls go to school.

Their hard-eyed leader remains a controversial figure in India with a list of criminal charges against her. She is a disruptor, a troublemaker, with thousands of detractors and even more admirers.

Sampat Pal Devi is not only one of the strongest women in India. She is one of the strongest women in the world.

Beet Risotto with Hazelnuts

YIELD: 4–6 SERVINGS

It's all about color and force. Sampat Pal Devi started a revolution with a bright pink sari and a bamboo stick in hand. Her girl gang grew as women joined her to march in the streets, sending a message to men that they could not intimidate women anymore. Like a fuchsia wave through the streets, their message was clear: *We're not backing down.*

So too with this recipe: the color alone will stop you in your tracks. The very word itself—*beet*—reminds us that we must not be cowed by violence. We fight fear with force. *You beat your wives, your children? We beet you right back down.* This risotto stands up and stands out, just like the ladies of the Gulabi Gang.

RECIPE

2 medium beets

2 tablespoons olive oil, divided

2 tablespoons unsalted butter

1 medium yellow onion, finely chopped

1 large clove fresh garlic, finely chopped

1 ¼ cups arborio rice

⅔ cup white wine

4 ½ cups water or stock

½ cup grated parmesan cheese

Sea salt and freshly cracked black pepper to taste

1 cup hazelnuts, toasted and roughly chopped

½ cup crumbled feta, goat cheese, or cubed pecorino

Handful of chopped flat-leaf parsley

SAVORY

- Preheat the oven to 375°F. Peel and trim the beets (use kitchen gloves if you don't want your hands to get stained), cut into large wedges, and place on a parchment-lined baking sheet. Toss with 1 tablespoon olive oil, season with a generous pinch of salt, then cook for 1 hour, until the beets are soft.

- Heat a large pan to medium-high heat, and add the remaining olive oil and butter. Tip in the onion and garlic, then cook for 3 to 5 minutes until translucent. Stir in the rice until well coated with the butter and oil. Add the white wine and stir until the wine is completely absorbed.

- Meanwhile, heat the water or stock in a medium pot until hot. Begin adding the hot liquid ½ cup at a time, stirring constantly and in the same direction, until absorbed, before adding the next ½ cup. Cook the rice until al dente (tender, but slightly chewy), about 20 minutes. All the hot liquid may not be needed to get your rice to the desired texture. Just continue to taste as you go.

- Puree ¼ of the cooked beets in a blender, and chop the remainder into small pieces. Stir the parmesan into the risotto, and season with salt and pepper. Add the beet puree and chopped beets, and stir to combine. Serve sprinkled with toasted hazelnuts, crumbled feta, and chopped parsley.

RECIPE PAIRING IDEA

This dish is filling on its own, but if you're going for a full, stunningly colorful spread, serve this rice alongside Rupi Kaur's refreshing Summer Shrub (page 208) and Ruth Coker Burks's Rainbow Salad (page 14).

The Question at the Table

What challenge in your life would you like to overcome, and
what are you willing to do to make that happen?

Sampat Pal Devi

GLORIA STEINEM

USA, 1934–

"This is no simple reform. It really is a revolution. Sex and race, because they are easy, visible differences, have been the primary ways of organizing human beings into superior and inferior groups, and into the cheap labor on which this system still depends. We are talking about a society in which there will be no roles other than those chosen, or those earned. We are really talking about humanism."

During a recent NPR interview, Gloria Steinem said that she is not an activist but a journalist. Far be it for us to differ with the glorious Ms. Steinem, but when you've had the kind of impact she's had, you stop being *just* anything. You are a force to be reckoned with, a name that has become synonymous with female empowerment.

But Gloria did indeed start as a journalist—and not the kind who writes about tidy, easily digestible things. No, her first serious assignment was an article about contraception. The piece, which appeared in *Esquire* in 1962, highlighted the ways in which women are forced to choose between marriage and career. Lest you think all Gloria did as a journalist was sit, call sources, and write, while working for *Show* magazine in 1963, she went undercover as a

Playboy bunny. Her article "A Bunny's Tale" revealed the exploitation and sexual demands—which either skirted or outright defied the law—bunnies were forced to face. Gloria received backlash for the article and was briefly unable to land further writing assignments.

At this point, Gloria was not yet a household name. Her 1969 article "After Black Power, Women's Liberation" brought her to national attention. Campaigning for the Equal Rights Amendment, she testified before the Senate Judiciary Committee in 1970.

We could go on and on (and on) about this wonderful woman, but the information is at your fingertips. What we'd like to end on is a bit of information you might miss if you're reading quickly through Gloria's Wikipedia entry: the first issue of *Ms.*—which Gloria cofounded in 1972, the three hundred thousand test copies of which sold out in eight days—featured five cover stories, two of which are as follows:

"Letty Pogrebin on Raising Kids without Sex Roles"
"Women Tell the Truth about Their Abortions"

These topics are still, in many places in this world, highly controversial. Women still suffer from prejudice and marginalization. But it's never too late to change that. Summon the spirit of 1972-era Gloria Steinem, and make your mark!

Caramelized Fennel Pasta

YIELD: 4 SERVINGS

Hold up. You say Gloria Steinem is pretty? Gorgeous, even? Well, you are right. Stunning in fact. But let's be clear, Gloria's physical beauty has no bearing—nope, none—on her contributions.

With that being said, we couldn't help but let our culinary imaginations run away with that *hair*—those highlights, that playful center part, the waves of '70s volume that frame her face.

"Spaghetti!" we said. Golden strands of semolina, cascading from your fork! From that initial

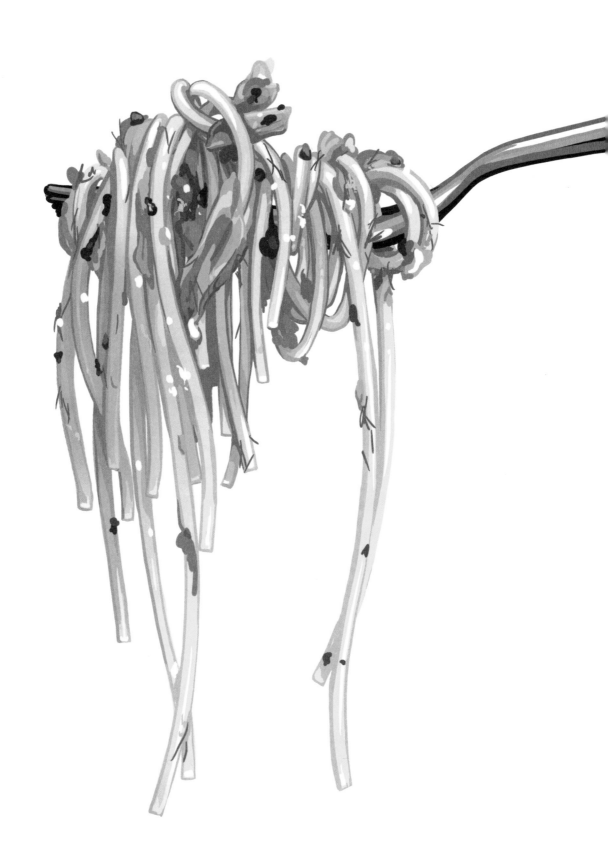

inspiration, we took a widely underrated vegetable—the mighty fennel—and caramelized it slowly, adding brightness with plenty of lemon, raw garlic, and fennel fronds at the end to make the dish pop.

So here are your orders for the day: go out and get yourself an iconic blowout and a copy of Gloria's memoir, and cozy up for a truly feisty feast.

RECIPE

2 medium bulbs fennel, with some tender green stems and fronds attached
½ teaspoon dried fennel seeds
¼ cup pine nuts
2 tablespoons unsalted butter, divided
2 tablespoons olive oil, divided
Sea salt and freshly cracked black pepper
1 medium shallot, thinly sliced
2 medium-large cloves fresh garlic, 1 thinly sliced and 1 smashed to a paste
1 lemon, zested and juiced separately
12 ounces spaghetti
3 to 4 tablespoons chopped Italian parsley
Finely shredded parmesan, pecorino, or other preferred hard cheese, as desired
Crushed red pepper flakes, as desired

- Remove the outer, tougher layers from the fennel bulbs if any. Chop the thinner stems and fronds to make ½ cup, and set aside for later. Halve the fennel bulbs, then thinly slice.

- Heat a large pan over medium-high heat, and toast the fennel seeds and pine nuts, moving the pan often to prevent browning, until the seeds are fragrant and the pine nuts have spots of color (you're not looking for the pine nuts to be completely toasted all the way through). Remove from the pan, place into the bowl of a mortar and pestle, and allow to cool.

- Bring the large pan back to high heat, and melt 1 tablespoon butter with 1 tablespoon olive oil. Add the shallot, thinly sliced garlic, and sliced fennel bulbs to the hot pan. Sprinkle with salt to begin layering the seasonings. Stir occasionally until the fennel begins to brown in places, about 7 to 10 minutes.

- Turn the heat down to medium-low, and add 1 cup water. Cover and cook until the liquid is mostly evaporated. Add another ½ cup water and the lemon juice, cover, and continue to cook until the fennel is soft and deep golden in color, about 20 minutes in all.

- Roughly pound the cooled fennel seeds and pine nuts with a mortar and pestle to break them up slightly, or chop by hand on a cutting board. Combine with the smashed garlic paste, remaining tablespoon of olive oil, and lemon zest. Season with salt and freshly cracked pepper, and stir in the reserved fennel fronds and stems to make a rough pesto mixture.

- Cook the spaghetti in salted water to al dente as directed on its packaging, reserving ½ cup of the pasta water. Combine the pasta with the caramelized fennel, and add the pesto mixture, chopped parsley, and enough pasta water to achieve desired creaminess. Top with cheese and red pepper flakes before serving.

RECIPE PAIRING IDEA

This pasta, like Gloria, stands out on its own. But to round this off as a meal, we suggest serving it with Buffy Sainte-Marie's Green Goddess Salad (page 2) or Chimamanda Ngozi Adichie's Salted Dark Chocolate Raspberry Tart (page 140).

The Question at the Table

When have you felt marginalized or less than? How did you respond?

BRENDA BERKMAN

USA, 1951–

> "In a small way, I was trying to challenge the stereotypes and fears that keep us from achieving our greatest potential. If I could be a firefighter—you can be anything."

Listen, we all love firefighters. Why not? They're tough, they're courageous, and a group of them shopping together is sure to contain one or two cuties.

But even our heroes can let us down. Take the case of the male firefighters who tried to keep Brenda Berkman from achieving her dream.

In 1977, the New York City Fire Department announced that it had opened up the firefighter exam to women. Brenda, a third-year law student, passed the written exam but failed the physical portion along with the eighty-nine other women who applied. An official later noted that the test was "the most difficult the department had ever administered...designed more to keep women out than to accurately assess job-related skills." Undeterred, Brenda requested a fairer test. She was ignored. In 1982, she filed a class-action lawsuit against the department, resulting in a new test based on job-related skills. Brenda, along with forty other women, passed the new test and entered the fire academy.

Yay! Brenda Berkman 1, FDNY 0. Except...

Within a year, Brenda was out of the job—fired for what the department claimed was lack of physical ability, despite coming in at the top of every task given to her. Her male colleagues clapped when she walked out of the firehouse. She and another female firefighter, Zaida

Gonzalez, sued to get their jobs back and won. In the ruling, the judge said the FDNY had failed to properly integrate women into its ranks. Additionally, he stated that Brenda and Zaida had been subjected to "extensive" sexual harassment.

For her first ten years, Brenda continued to experience harassment. Denied mentoring or even words exchanged with her peers, she had to be more aware than any other firefighter just to do her job. Piss in her boots, hidden uniforms, giant bras hung over her locker—she persisted through it all, because she didn't want other female firefighters to suffer similar abuses.

Brenda is the definition of *hero* in more than just feisty ways. Off duty when the first plane hit the north World Trade Center tower on September 11, 2001, she nonetheless ran to the nearest firehouse, arriving at the site just as the north tower collapsed. For that whole day and the weeks that followed, she searched for survivors and remains. She later pushed for the female firefighters and others who responded during and after 9/11 to be acknowledged.

Still a vocal advocate for gender equality, Brenda's efforts are a perfect illustration of not backing down—not from a system rigged against you, not from an entire skyscraper crumbling before you.

Pork Winter Squash Ragù

YIELD: 12–14 SERVINGS

Don't know if you know this, buuuuuut...firefighters eat a *lot*. Like, a *table full of growing adolescents lot*. No surprise then that meals in the firehouse are a big part of being a firefighter, building a firefighting community.

During meals, we should forgive others' trespasses and ignore what separates us. For many years, though, Brenda was denied this experience. She was kept apart from others, made to feel like an outsider. Peanut butter and jelly sandwiches were her staple while she sat alone. Did it make her any less effective? No. Did she knock down every obstacle in her way regardless of this insult? Yes.

Still. She should have been at the table, cracking jokes, sharing stories of heroism, breaking bread *together*. And while firehouses are still plagued with traditions of frat-style hazing and overwhelming toxic masculinity, they are thankfully less so because of Brenda.

Brenda Berkman

We created a meal for her and the family she eventually found—the community firefighters pride themselves in.

This recipe yield is larger than the others, so make note that you may need to make room in your freezer for leftovers. (But if there are firefighters eating with you, don't worry—there won't be any leftovers.)

RECIPE

2 pounds kabocha, butternut, or acorn squash
½ pound bacon, chopped
1 cup olive oil
1 ¼ cups finely chopped celery
2 cups finely chopped onion
2 cups finely chopped carrots
1 cup finely chopped leeks
4 large cloves fresh garlic, chopped
2 pounds ground pork
2 teaspoons sea salt, plus more for seasoning
Freshly cracked black pepper
1 bay leaf
1 whole chile de árbol (or other small hot red pepper)
4 cups chicken stock (and more as necessary)
1 heaping tablespoon chopped fresh thyme
1 heaping tablespoon chopped fresh rosemary
3 ½ pounds pasta of choice
2 tablespoons apple cider vinegar
2 tablespoons balsamic vinegar
Parmesan or pecorino cheese, finely grated, as desired
Crushed red pepper flakes (optional)

- Preheat the oven to 375°F, and line a sheet tray with parchment paper. Halve the squash, and scoop out the seeds. Place the squash skin side up on the sheet tray, and roast for 25 to 30 minutes. Toast until tender when pierced with a paring knife in the thickest part of the squash.

- Let the cooked squash cool, then scoop out the orange flesh into a medium-sized bowl, and mash it well with the back of a fork to break up some of the large chunks. Set aside.

- Heat a large, heavy-bottomed pot (a Dutch oven works nicely) on medium-high, and add the bacon, stirring often until most of the fat has rendered and the proteins begin to brown, about 5 to 8 minutes. Remove from the pot, and set aside.

- Add the olive oil, followed by celery, onion, carrot, and leeks. Cook on medium, stirring often for a good 30 to 40 minutes. This here is your sofrito—the flavor backbone of the ragù. Adjust the temperature as needed to keep the sofrito sizzling and not browning too much.

- Add the garlic and the pork. Season with salt and pepper, and stir often to break up the clusters of ground pork and for everything to cook evenly.

- Add the mashed squash, bay leaf, chili pepper, stock, thyme, and rosemary. Turn the temperature to low, and simmer for at least 1 hour (ideally 3 to 4 hours on low, adding water occasionally if it looks dry). The ragù will reduce and thicken during this time. Continue stirring occasionally, maintaining a constant simmer.

- To serve, boil a large pot of well-salted water, and cook your favorite pasta al dente (we love this with rigatoni, but any shape will work).

- Remove the bay leaf and chile from the ragù, while adding in the vinegars.

- Check the seasoning of salt and pepper.

- Serve topped with grated cheese and red pepper flakes if desired.

RECIPE PAIRING IDEA

This big pot of ragù is really the ultimate comfort food. Serve it with a side of Buffy Sainte-Marie's Green Goddess Salad (page 2), and end the meal with the Queen of Soul, Aretha Franklin, and her sexy skillet of Peaches and Biscuits (page 158). Respect really is delicious.

The Question at the Table

What traditions or memories do you remember from sharing food around the table with others?

Brenda Berkman

TAWAKKOL KARMAN

YEMEN, 1979–

> "The solution to women's issues can only be achieved in a free and democratic society in which human energy is liberated, the energy of both women and men together. Our civilization is called human civilization and is not attributed only to men or women."

Never underestimate the power of *no*. It is a deceptively simple statement—a simple word you learn early and then take for granted. For many women around the world, however, *no* is not a right. In a variety of circumstances, refusal is not an option.

Meet Yemeni human rights advocate Tawakkol Karman. She is a Nobel Peace Prize laureate, a journalist, a mother, and one of the toughest women to ever live. Future generations might well call her the "Queen of No," but her current monikers—"Mother of the Revolution" and "Iron Woman"—are spot-on too.

"My father taught me to say no, and to question everything that my mind or heart did not accept. He taught me to be in the front line, not to fear anyone, and not to wait for solutions from others or to expect help from anyone, including my brothers."

Not only has Tawakkol placed herself, again and again, in the center of Yemeni politics (very much not the traditional place for women in Yemen; before her, no woman's image had ever been used to protest government corruption in the country), but in 2005, she cofounded

Women Journalists Without Chains, which advocates for freedom of expression and democratic ideals.

Beginning in 2007, Tawakkol led protests against the Saleh regime, becoming a pivotal figure in the Arab Spring movement. By early 2011, she was arrested and jailed for her disruptive efforts, only to be released within weeks when the nation overthrew Saleh.

Unfortunately for the people of Yemen, saying no to injustice has come with a cost. There as elsewhere, the fight against corruption is seen as a threat to old orders. Factions bent on destabilizing the region—Houthi rebels and Iran on one side, Saudi Arabia and the United Arab Emirates on the other—are right now waging a war on Yemeni soil.

Tawakkol is unbowed, defiant: "Our destiny is to win, and our promise is to establish the state of right and law—we did not surrender, and we will not. The morning of our dreams will come true."

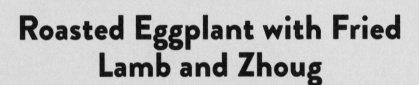

Roasted Eggplant with Fried Lamb and Zhoug

YIELD: 4–6 SERVINGS

Iron. Woman. What on earth do you pair with someone as tough as Tawakkol Karman? Something big, definitely. Something bold and *spicy*.

Thankfully, a Yemeni woman is no stranger to spice. In fact, Yemen is not only the birthplace of Tawakkol but the origin of zhoug, one of our very favorite condiments. Think of it as the powerful, sexy, and spicy neighbor of pesto—tons of fresh cilantro, cumin seeds, cardamom, and loads of heat from fresh chilies.

Just like the mark that Tawakkol has left on the world, we hope this recipe and its special spicy sauce will become a staple of your meant-to-impress meals.

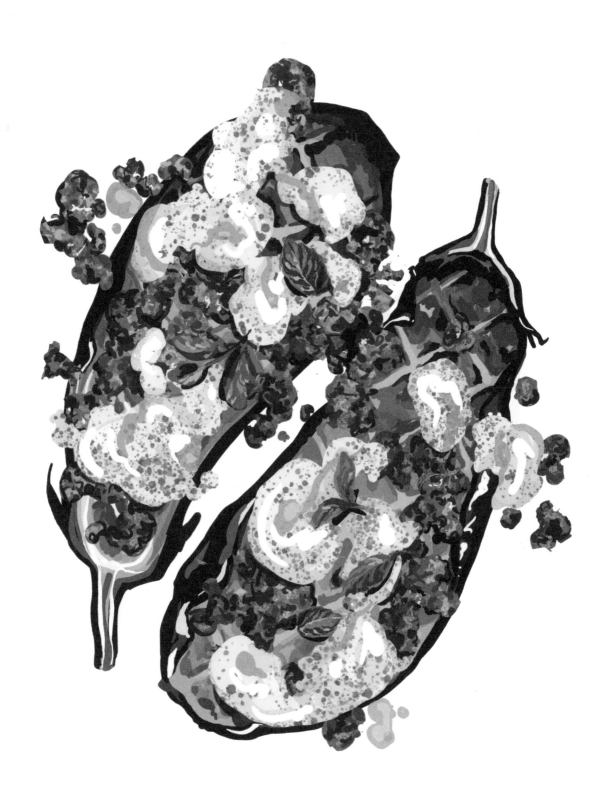

The eggplant not only looks striking, but the method of roasting them halved leaves the center almost jammy and fluffy with a slight bitterness from the chewy skin. If eggplant isn't your most loved vegetable, though, don't be discouraged! You can easily swap it out with zucchini or even a winter squash, and it'll be just as good.

RECIPE

4 to 5 small-medium eggplants (about 2 pounds), halved lengthwise

3 tablespoons olive oil, plus more for drizzling

1 medium onion, thinly sliced

1 clove fresh garlic, smashed into a paste

1 pound ground lamb

1 teaspoon ground cumin

3 teaspoons smoked paprika

½ teaspoon ground ginger

1 teaspoon sea salt

Freshly cracked black pepper

1 tablespoon sesame seeds

¼ cup golden raisins, chopped

Juice of ½ lemon

1 cup labneh or whole milk Greek yogurt

Mint and cilantro leaves for garnish

Flaky salt to finish (optional)

- Preheat the oven to 425°F. Use the sharp tip of a paring knife to make ½-inch slits in the cut sides of the eggplant. Place the eggplants skin side down on a baking tray, drizzle with olive oil, sprinkle with salt and pepper, and then turn cut side down. Roast for 30 to 40 minutes (depending on the size of eggplants). Check for doneness by poking with a paring knife. It should be extremely tender, and the dark skin will look slightly shriveled.

- Heat the olive oil in a large skillet over medium-high heat, and add the onion. Stir often with a wooden spoon, and just as the onion starts to show signs of color on some edges, add the garlic, followed by the ground lamb, spices, salt, pepper, and sesame seeds. Stir often, and watch for the meat to begin to brown and crisp up around the edges, about 8 to 10 minutes. Stir in the chopped raisins and lemon juice just before you're ready to serve.

- Mix the labneh with 2 to 4 tablespoons zhoug (see recipe below; this all depends on the heat of your chilies and your personal spice preference).

Tawakkol Karman

- To serve, set the roasted eggplants on a plate or platter, and pour the lamb over the top. Add dollops of zhoug labneh, drizzle with more olive oil, and sprinkle with torn mint and cilantro leaves and flaky salt.

ZHOUG

¼ cup olive oil

1 bunch cilantro, small stems okay

½ bunch flat-leaf parsley

2 tablespoons lemon juice

2 to 3 jalapeño peppers, sliced

2 large cloves fresh garlic

1 teaspoon ground cumin

1 teaspoon sugar

½ teaspoon Aleppo pepper or crushed red pepper flakes

½ teaspoon ground cardamom

½ teaspoon sea salt

- Mix all ingredients in a food processor until desired texture is reached. We like it best when it mimics a slightly chunky pesto, as opposed to a creamy sauce, but make it your own! Add spoonfuls of water if you need to thin it out.

RECIPE PAIRING IDEA
Round out this dish into a complete and filling meal by bringing in Wangari Maathai's Celery Root and Pecan Salad (page 28) and a refreshing side of Rupi Kaur's Summer Shrub (page 208) with ginger beer.

SAVORY

The Question at the Table

You may not be referred to as the "Iron Woman," but if you could choose a nickname for yourself, what would it be?

Tawakkol Karman

JUNKO TABEI

JAPAN, 1939–2016

"Technique and ability alone do not get you to the top—it is the willpower that is the most important. This willpower you cannot buy with money or be given by others—it rises from your heart."

If you're four foot eleven, chances are you're as used to being underestimated as you are to proving people wrong. A person's capability is not the same as a person's *size*—a fact demonstrated by Junko Tabei, one of Japan's most celebrated mountain climbers.

"Anyone with a pair of feet who can walk can climb," Junko Tabei once said, showing characteristic humility despite the facts of her incredible life.

Fascinated with climbing even as a child, she had long set her sights peak-high. But cultural norms—what a woman could or could not do in her culture—placed many obstacles along her ascent. This did not shake Junko's focus. She was small, but she was born to conquer giants.

In 1969, Junko formed the Ladies Climbing Club in response to mistreatment by male mountaineers of the time, setting the route for her greatest accomplishment—becoming the first woman to stand on the roof of the world. She spent years in preparation for Everest, working as an editor, piano teacher, and English instructor to raise funds.

All the same, she didn't do it alone. In 1975, Junko led fifteen Ladies Climbing Club members on an expedition to Everest. Along the route, an avalanche buried her completely, and she lost consciousness for six minutes. She recovered, ascending to the 29,035-foot summit. Every one of her climbing partners followed, without a single casualty.

As if that wasn't enough, Junko went on to ascend all Seven Summits, the highest peak on each continent—the first woman to do so. She then went a step further, becoming a powerful advocate for mountain environments as she witnessed the rapid commercialization of Everest. Shocked and heartbroken by the impact of human waste on the world's most respected mountaintops, she returned to university for a postgrad degree in environmental science. Before her death in 2016, she led an annual trip with high school students to the peak of Mount Fuji and ascended the loftiest peaks in Luxembourg, Belgium, and Niger. Imagine what it must have been like to see her in her element, the air thinning, the visibility hazing, her powerful legs growing heavy. These moments, when she struggled and persevered against the earth and sky and mankind, solidified her legacy—she became colossal, as mighty a force as the mountains themselves.

Junko Tabei

Bold Peanutty Shrimp

YIELD: 4 SERVINGS

Size smashes expectations all the time. With bold ambition, even the tiniest of creatures can manage the miraculous. (Look at the mighty ant, the blurred-wing hummingbird—the hardy tardigrade!) Junko proved that and multiplied it by seven.

This vibrant dish zooms in on shrimp (but don't call them shrimpy!) that show up big and strong on the plate. The sweet and spicy marinade caramelizes beautifully on the grill, scattered with crunchy peanuts, and a heavy hand of fresh herbs takes this dish to the next level.

We'd love to sit with Junko, a cold beer, and a plate of shrimp in hand, listening to tales from the top of the world.

RECIPE

3 tablespoons grape-seed oil

1 tablespoon Worcestershire sauce

6 cloves fresh garlic

3 long red sweet/spicy chili peppers (Fresno chilies, for example)

1 shallot, roughly chopped

¼ cup sugar

1 teaspoon sea salt

Freshly cracked black pepper

2 pounds large shrimp (16 to 20 count), peeled and deveined

1 cup basil and cilantro leaves, torn (optional)

½ cup roasted peanuts, chopped (optional)

Lime wedges

Cooked rice for serving

- Combine the oil, Worcestershire sauce, garlic, chili pepper, shallots, sugar, salt, and black pepper in a blender. You can adjust the spiciness to your liking by using less or more chilies and less or more sugar if you prefer. Blend until smooth.

- Combine the shrimp with the marinade in a bowl. Make sure all the shrimp are well coated, and refrigerate for 30 minutes to 2 hours.

- Heat the grill to high heat. Grill the shrimp until pink and caramelized on the edges from the grill, 1 to 2 minutes per side. While still hot from the grill, top with torn herbs, chopped peanuts, and a squeeze of lime as desired. Serve with fluffy, hot white rice.

NOTE: *If shellfish isn't for you, worry not! Try this marinade on chicken wings! Start out by broiling salt and pepper seasoned wings for 10 minutes per side until golden. Then toss the wings in this spicy marinade before finishing under the broiler for 5 more minutes.*

RECIPE PAIRING IDEA

When wondering what to serve alongside this spicy shrimp dish, consider inviting Qiu Jin and her refreshing Lemony Smashed Cucumber Salad (page 20) to join, and finish off the meal with Jane Goodall's Palm Sugar Banana Bread (page 178).

The Question at the Table

What physical activity would you like to try your
hand at? What's holding you back?

DICKEY CHAPELLE

USA, C. 1919–1965

"It is not a woman's place. There's no question about it. There's only one other species on earth for whom a war zone is no place, and that's men. But as long as men continue to fight wars, why I think observers of both sexes will be sent to see what happens."

First, a dose of reality. Women have always inhabited war zones. They have fought, they have defended, they have died.

Before Dickey Chapelle, though, women didn't typically chronicle warfare. In 1945, she—twenty-seven years old, divorced, with few photo credits to her name and no experience of warfare—became a war correspondent photojournalist for *National Geographic*, covering the battles of Iwo Jima and Okinawa.

Think about that. This small woman ventured into two of the most chaotic places in the world. History would forgive anyone for saying, "Yup. Tried that and it was hell. Going back home."

Dickey had other plans. From Japan, she dedicated her life to documenting the horrors of warfare, suffering with men half her age—sleeping in the mud, slogging through freezing rain, coming under fire. She kept her cool dressed in her signature uniform: fatigues, bush hat, cat's-eye glasses, and pearl earrings.

In 1956, she was held in solitary confinement in Hungary for over seven weeks. She earned the respect of the troops with whom she traveled. After training with the Screaming Eagles paratroopers, she became the only woman authorized to jump into combat in Vietnam.

In 1965, while on patrol with a Marine platoon, the lieutenant before her kicked a tripwire booby trap, mortally wounding Dickey. In an evac helicopter above Chu Lai, Vietnam, she told a crewman, "I guess it was bound to happen."

Of course, we like to think such events are not *bound* to happen. Thanks to women like Dickey, who spend their lives revealing the horrors of war to those lucky enough to find safety, our world may yet achieve peace.

Dickey Chapelle

Potato-Crusted Salmon with Dill and Sour Cream

Dickey called Milwaukee home. In that particular part of the country, being of German heritage means knowing something about potatoes and mustard—staples in Germanic cooking. We made sure to incorporate both in this outrageously savory dish: fine potato chips, crushed and combined with fresh herbs, adhered to the delicious pink flesh of salmon with—you guessed it—mustard. Avoid individual salmon filets; this is a meal to be shared with a table full of friends.

And what do friends do when they eat? They tell stories. Pause a moment during this meal, and bow your heads briefly for Dickey Chapelle. Imagine being brave enough to jump into the howling wind, poised above an alien landscape, knowing what may lie below among those trees—to stare violence down through the lens of a camera, and to not once forget to put in your pearl earrings.

That, friends, is a story worthy of a good meal.

To Dickey! To *peace*!

RECIPE

1 side of salmon (about 3 pounds)
Sea salt and freshly cracked black pepper
¼ cup Dijon mustard
1 (5.5-ounce) bag quality salted potato chips
Zest of ½ lemon, plus the remainder of the lemon for serving
¼ cup chopped fresh dill, divided
2 tablespoons olive oil
1 cup sour cream

- Preheat the oven to 400°F. Line a baking sheet with parchment paper.

- Lay the side of salmon, skin side down, in the center of the baking sheet. Season it lightly with salt and pepper, and smear on the Dijon mustard.

- Crush the potato chips in a ziplock bag with a rolling pin until pea-size or smaller. Add to a bowl along with the lemon zest and half the dill. Mix in the oil until incorporated.

- Coat the salmon with a thin, even layer of potato chip crumbs. Pat them on the fish gently so they stay put.

- Bake for about 20 to 25 minutes, or until the chip coating is nicely browned. Use 2 spatulas to transfer the salmon to a serving platter, putting one at either end and lifting them up together so the salmon is in one piece. Lay it gently on the serving platter, and put a large fork and spoon on the table by the platter so that people can serve themselves. You can also serve the salmon right on the baking sheet—there's no shame in that.

- Mix the remaining dill in a bowl with the sour cream, and serve on the side with wedges of the lemon used for zest.

RECIPE PAIRING IDEA

When preparing to serve this salmon, consider inviting a side dish to accompany it. We think either Leymah Gbowee's Spice Roasted Sweet Potatoes with Yogurt and Cilantro (page 8) or Oprah Winfrey's Purple Potato Salad with Fried Capers (page 52) could beautifully complete this perfect potato-centric feast!

The Question at the Table

**Bravery comes in all shapes and sizes.
When was a time you felt brave?**

Dickey Chapelle

MALALA YOUSAFZAI

PAKISTAN, 1997–

"If one man can destroy everything, why can't one girl change it?"

Don't let *Malala* become just a name. Certainly, let us never forget what she stands for: the rights of girls—no, *everyone*—to receive an education.

Born in 1997 in the Swat Valley, Khyber Pakhtunkhwa, Pakistan, Malala came to value education at an early age. Her father, who managed a number of schools, encouraged all his children to pursue education despite the social structures set in place to discourage girls from going to school.

At eleven years old, Malala wrote a pseudonymous blog post for BBC Urdu that detailed her life under recent Taliban rule, which included a ban on education for girls. The next summer, journalist Adam B. Ellick filmed a *New York Times* documentary about her.

The Taliban would allow no *girl* to receive such attention for defying them. On October 9, 2012, a Taliban gunman shot Malala and two other girls in retaliation for her activism. Struck in the head, Malala nonetheless recovered—*and* became the world's most prominent advocate for the right to education.

At sixteen, she coauthored *I Am Malala*, an international bestseller recounting her experiences, and founded the Malala Fund, a nonprofit organization that fights for girls' access to education. As a result of her advocacy, Malala was the corecipient of the 2014 Nobel Peace Prize, making her, at seventeen, the youngest-ever Nobel Prize laureate.

"I tell my story not because it is unique, but because it is the story of many girls," Malala said. "We need to encourage girls that their voice matters. I think there are hundreds and thousands of Malalas out there."

Now, *you there*, reading this, go, make food, recite poetry, share stories, and celebrate accomplishments with the girls in your life. Show them how much joy there is in learning about the wonderful world we can build together.

In short, be a Malala.

Malala Yousafzai

Cardamom Spiced Roasted Chicken

YIELD: 4–6 SERVINGS

It is said that Malala has the golden pen, with which she wrote of the injustice against girls, advocating for their equal right to learn. With the heavy hand of truth, she shared her story, even though it meant being targeted by hate.

Here we have a recipe of strong Pakistani flavors, the very spices Malala grew up with: cardamom, black pepper, cumin, and coriander. We use our own heavy hands, wielding a mortar and pestle of truthful flavor to crush the whole, toasted spices into a fragrant powder. It is important not to skip this step; don't go for the already-ground spice options, which would dilute the fragrant appeal of this delicious golden chicken dish.

It's worth seeking out a spatchcocked chicken or learning to do it yourself with the help of the Internet and a heavy knife. The benefit of this is the expansion of visible surface area (e.g., crispier chicken skin!). Enough said. The outcome really is a stunning centerpiece to bring friends and family together.

RECIPE

Seeds from 10 cardamom pods

2 teaspoons black peppercorns

2 teaspoons whole coriander

2 teaspoons cumin seeds

1 teaspoon Aleppo chili or crushed red pepper flakes (optional)

4 teaspoons sea salt

4 cloves fresh garlic

2 tablespoons olive oil

1 cup whole milk Greek yogurt, or coconut milk yogurt

2 tablespoons grated fresh ginger

2 tablespoons freshly squeezed lemon juice

1 (3- to 4-pound) chicken, spatchcocked or cut in half
    by your butcher
Fresh cilantro leaves and lime wedges for garnish

- Grind the cardamom seeds, peppercorns, coriander, cumin, and chili in a mortar with pestle to a fine powder. Add the salt and garlic, and smash the garlic well. Add the olive oil to form a paste. Stir this mixture with the yogurt, ginger, and lemon juice in a small bowl.

- Place the chicken in a large bowl or pan. Start by rubbing the yogurt mixture between the skin and the meat of the chicken. Get it everywhere! Then smear the remaining yogurt over the outside of the chicken, front and back, nice and thick. Refrigerate for at least 8 hours or up to 24 hours. Remove the chicken from the refrigerator 30 minutes before roasting.

- Preheat the oven to 425°F. Place the chicken breast side up in a baking pan or cast iron pan. Bake in the oven until thoroughly cooked, 45 minutes to 1 hour. Remove and let rest 15 minutes before carving. Serve garnished with cilantro leaves and lime wedges, and remember to pour the leftover juices from the pan back over the chicken.

RECIPE PAIRING IDEA

This chicken dish shines bright as a centerpiece and can be combined with nearly anything. We particularly love it with Qiu Jin's Lemony Smashed Cucumber Salad (page 20) and Angela Davis's Spiced Molasses Cake with Crunchy Lemon Glaze (page 170).

The Question at the Table

If money, time, and privilege were no consideration, what would you most like to study or simply take a class on?

Malala Yousafzai

HEDY LAMARR

USA, 1914–2000

> "Analysis gave me great freedom of emotions and fantastic confidence. I felt I had served my time as a puppet."

Hedwig Eva Maria Kiesler—Hedy—lived a childhood straight out of legend. Born into a well-to-do Jewish family, she was the only child of doting parents. Her mother, a skilled pianist, brought the arts into their home. Her father was a successful banker who adored his daughter. They walked the streets, discussing how the streetcar functioned or questioning the mechanics of various machines.

Hedy was a natural beauty, with dark eyebrows, a bright complexion, and deep knowing in her eyes. She was smart, incredibly so, but her brilliance was often ignored, and her beauty took center stage.

An acting career soon developed. Fate took her from small roles in Vienna to Berlin, where she encountered Nazism and fled to Britain. By the time she reached the United States, she had changed her name to Hedy Lamarr and convinced the head of MGM to sign her on. From the late 1930s and into the '50s, she was in dozens of Hollywood films, teamed up with some of the era's most famous stars.

She was famous for her looks, smoldering eyes, and bombshell allure, but her greatest contribution had nothing to do with sex appeal.

In the lead-up to World War II, her body and mind sprang into action. She lent her image to the war effort and worked at the Hollywood Canteen, a restaurant-bar set up in the heart of Los Angeles as a send-off for servicemen leaving for the war. She nearly quit showbiz to help the war effort.

Instead, she began inventing, and her focus quickly turned to military applications.

In 1941, Hedy and coinventor George Antheil invented radio communications technology that "hopped" from one frequency to another, allowing Allied torpedoes to escape detection. Though not utilized until well after the war, the patent they filed was a precursor to secure Wi-Fi, GPS, and Bluetooth technology now used by billions of people around the world. Unfortunately, neither inventor received formal recognition for their invention.

The incredible thing about it all? Hedy had no formal training as an inventor. Her entire career was built on her looks—her job was in front of the camera. "Any girl can be glamorous. All you have to do is stand still and look stupid," she once said. Thankfully, our girl wasn't content to just *stand still*. She wielded her fame and resources to support her true passion.

She played the acting role, and played it well, but no script could hold back Hedy Lamarr.

Vibrant Lemon Poppy Seed Bundt Cake

YIELD: 8–10 SERVINGS

Even now, female actors have to fight to be recognized for their intellects. All the same, time has proven we're determined to break the cycle of toxic masculinity that defines us by our appearance. We will be recognized for our outward *and* inward beauty—our grace and our intelligence in equal measure.

So here we are, crowning the queen of both beauty and brains, with a Bundt cake that is both

attractive and delicious. This cake is vibrant and zesty, boldly colored with a touch of turmeric and freckled with poppy seeds.

In Austria, the Bundt cake is famous, known as *Gugelhupf*. We like to picture Hedy and her father stopping in an elegantly mirrored pastry shop after one of their walks: They sit, grinning at each other over slices of cake. They talk about the world as they take their first joyous bites. They discuss how things work—the traffic lights, the trolleys, maybe even beauty itself.

RECIPE

4 tablespoons lemon zest (about 4 lemons)

2 cups sugar

18 tablespoons (2 ¼ sticks) unsalted butter, softened

3 cups all-purpose flour

1 teaspoon baking powder

½ teaspoon baking soda

½ teaspoon ground turmeric

½ teaspoon sea salt

3 tablespoons poppy seeds

4 eggs

¾ cup buttermilk

4 tablespoons lemon juice

1 teaspoon vanilla extract (see recipe on page 191 for a homemade version)

- Preheat the oven to 350°F. Butter and flour a Bundt pan; a good trick is to mix 1 tablespoon flour with 1 tablespoon melted butter. Use a pastry brush to apply the paste to all the curves of your Bundt pan.

- Massage the lemon zest and sugar together with your fingertips in a medium bowl until the sugar is completely fragrant with bruised zest.

- Beat the lemon sugar and butter together in a standing mixer fitted with a paddle attachment until pale and fluffy, about 3 minutes.

- Combine the flour, baking powder, baking soda, turmeric, salt, and poppy seeds together in a medium bowl, and set aside.

- Combine the eggs, buttermilk, lemon juice, and vanilla in a liquid measuring cup, and give it a little whisk to break up the eggs.

- Alternately add the dry and wet ingredients in 3 additions to the butter mixture on low speed. Be sure to incorporate but not overmix. Scrape down the bowl as needed.

- Pour the batter into the prepared pan, and smooth the top with a rubber spatula. Bake the cake for 45 to 50 minutes or until the top is golden brown and a skewer inserted into the center comes out clean.

- Let the cake cool for 15 minutes in the Bundt pan. Use a toothpick to poke many tiny holes on the surface as it cools. Use a pastry brush to brush lemon syrup (recipe below) over the surface, then invert the cake onto a platter. Brush the remaining exposed surface with lemon syrup; be generous for maximum lemon flavor!

LEMON SYRUP

½ cup sugar
¼ cup lemon juice (2 lemons)

- Bring the sugar and lemon juice to a boil in a small saucepan, stirring occasionally to dissolve the sugar. Reduce heat to low, and simmer until the liquid has thickened slightly (about 2 minutes).

RECIPE PAIRING IDEA

One of the beautiful things about a cake like this is its versatility, making it perfect for nearly any time of day. Pair it with Marsha P. Johnson's Golden Baked Eggs for brunch (page 76), or enjoy it alongside a cup of coffee or Amelia Earhart's Rich Hot Chocolate (page 202) in the afternoon.

The Question at the Table

When have you felt that one of your strengths has been overlooked
due to others' preconceived notions about you?

CHIMAMANDA NGOZI ADICHIE

NIGERIA, 1977–

> "Of course I am not worried about intimidating men. The type of man who will be intimidated by me is exactly the type of man I have no interest in."

Growing up in Nigeria, Chimamanda Ngozi Adichie pored over American and British books. In her justly celebrated 2009 TED talk, "The Danger of a Single Story," Chimamanda said, "They stirred my imagination and opened up new worlds for me. But the unintended consequence was that I did not know that people like me could exist in literature."

At nineteen, Chimamanda dropped out of medical school and left Nigeria to study in the United States, bringing her face-to-face with true American racism. Judged for being an immigrant and a dark-skinned woman, she struggled to define herself through the written word. And define herself she did!

However much we don't want to relegate Chimamanda's writing to a single theme (don't worry; we'll get to another important one in just a sec!), we would be remiss to ignore the importance of her work in light of race. We need to hear from such brave, strong women of color in order to shift American literary culture.

It's difficult to envision the #ownvoices hashtag, which emphasizes the rights of people of color to tell stories informed by their individual experiences, existing without Chimamanda. She is a force for good like few authors before her.

Chimamanda also speaks frankly about gender and family dynamics. Though married, she prefers to be called "Miss" and did not take her husband's surname, insisting that a woman should not be compelled to abandon her own name. She insists on a true domestic balance, saying that "when there is true equality in the home, resentment does not exist."

One of Chimamanda's most recent works, a book-length essay titled *Dear Ijeawele, or A Feminist Manifesto in Fifteen Suggestions*, is inspired by a letter she wrote to a friend asking for advice on how to raise a daughter as a feminist. It's a sad, joyous, searing, heartfelt work, full of advice our mothers and girls need to hear:

"Teach her to reject likability. Her job is not to make herself likable, her job is to be her full self, a self that is honest and aware of the equal humanity of other people."

Salted Dark Chocolate Raspberry Tart

YIELD: 8–10 SERVINGS

If you have not indulged in Chimamanda's books yet, get yourself to your local bookstore stat! Aside from the brilliant writing, poignant details, and relevant themes, Chimamanda writes challenging books that leave readers speechless, their heads filled with new ideas.

We were inspired to make a recipe for the exact coffee table treat we crave while reading her work: a dark chocolate tart studded with flaky salt, hovering over a sandy crust with a tangy

layer of raspberry jam. It's the kind of dessert you want to drop off to your daughter in her new apartment, the fledgling mother down the hall, or your niece on her way off to college.

As long as you're bringing the tart, why not pick up that dog-eared copy of *Americanah* and share it too?

CRUST

1 cup ground almonds
1 cup all-purpose flour (or gluten-free all-purpose flour)
½ cup sugar
¼ teaspoon sea salt
½ teaspoon almond extract (optional)
8 tablespoons unsalted butter, cubed and at room temperature

- Add the ground almonds, flour, sugar, and salt to the bowl of a food processor, and pulse 3 or 4 times to combine. Continue to pulse while adding the soft butter one cube at a time. The mixture is ready when the dough looks moist but still sandy and has not quite joined together in a big ball. Pour the sandy mixture out into a 9-inch tart pan with a removable bottom. Press with your hands to fill the pan evenly. You'll need about half the dough for the edges and the other half for the middle. Prick the crust all over with a fork, and set on a sheet pan in the freezer for 30 minutes up to several days.

- Preheat the oven to 350°F. Take the sheet pan with the crust from the freezer straight to the oven, and bake for 25 minutes, until the edges begin to turn golden in color. Set aside to cool while you prepare the filling.

FILLING

½ cup raspberry jam
1 cup whole milk (or milk alternative)
Pinch of sea salt
9 ounces (1 ½ cups) dark (70%) chocolate, roughly chopped
1 teaspoon unsalted butter, room temperature
1 teaspoon vanilla extract (see recipe on page 191 for a homemade version)
Flaky salt to finish
Optional garnishes of cocoa powder, chopped almonds, or crumbled
　　freeze-dried raspberries

Chimamanda Ngozi Adichie

- Warm the jam in a small pot over medium heat. Stir often to prevent it from burning on the bottom, and continue cooking as it begins to bubble for 1 minute. Let cool, then pour on top of the baked and cooled tart shell, and spread out evenly. Place in the fridge until the chocolate filling is ready.

- Combine the milk and pinch of salt in a small pot over medium heat, and stir with a wire whisk to prevent sticking. Remove from the heat just as it begins to boil, and immediately add the chopped chocolate. Cover the pot with a lid, and let sit for 2 minutes. Remove the lid, and whisk well to incorporate the chocolate until smooth. Whisk in the butter and vanilla extract, until shiny and glossy.

- Pour the chocolate mixture over the jam layer in the crust. Place the tart in the fridge to cool completely for at least 1 hour.

- To serve, sprinkle the tart with good flaky salt and any other garnish you choose. It's best to cut the tart using a knife warmed in hot water.

RECIPE PAIRING IDEA

This tart would be the perfect ending to any meal at your table. But we would love to invite legends like Ina May Gaskin and her Little Bean Soup with Rosemary Salsa Verde (page 86) and Wangari Maathai's Celery Root and Pecan Salad (page 28) to the table.

The Question at the Table

If you could pass on one piece of advice to a friend raising a daughter, what would you like to convey? Remember, you don't have to be a parent to give helpful tips!

SOPHIE SCHOLL

GERMANY, 1921–1943

"Stand up for what you believe in even if you are standing alone."

Our leaders shouldn't have to become martyrs in order for us to learn from them. Our leaders should be celebrated while they live.

However, if one must die for a cause, *it should be for something like fighting Nazis.*

Sophie Scholl died before her twenty-second birthday, executed in 1943 by the Nazi regime for high treason after being caught distributing antiwar pamphlets at the University of Munich. Her coconspirators—her brother Hans, twenty-four, and their best friend, Christoph Probst, twenty-two—were murdered by guillotine alongside her.

If we stopped with this, however, we'd be doing Sophie a huge disservice, for her story is equal parts courage *and* redemption.

As a child and young woman, she had been a member of the girl's branch of the Hitler Youth. She and her brother often tangled horns with their father, a staunch opponent of the Nazi regime.

Sophie remained largely sympathetic to Nazism well into her teens, within sight of her own death. But things slowly shifted as she attended university and learned more about the realities and atrocities taking place on the Eastern Front. And then, in 1941, her father was arrested for "treachery." Sophie could no longer keep silent. She became a member of the White Rose, a resistance group of University of Munich students who began distributing flyers against the deportation of Jews to concentration camps. Their audience started small, but thousands of pamphlets were eventually distributed, reaching households across Germany.

Their message grew as well, eventually advocating for the sabotage of Hitler and his war machine.

On February 18, 1943, in what we can only assume was an attempt to reach more readers, Sophie pushed a stack of White Rose pamphlets off the top banister of the university's central hall. This scene was reported by a janitor, leading to Sophie and Hans's arrest by the Gestapo.

Before her trial, Sophie was "interrogated" for seventeen hours. Surely, she suspected her fate. Rather than be cowed, she used this moment to interrupt the judge, to speak truth to power.

"Somebody had to make a start!" she shouted. "What we said and wrote are what many people are thinking. They just don't dare say it out loud!"

Though none of us wish for a similar fate, Sophie's life is a lesson to us all: *It is never too late to fight your programming, to do the right thing.*

White Rose Butter Cookies

YIELD: 30–35 COOKIES

Tradition is a double-edged sword. Following the traditions of Nazi-era Germany, the brainwashing of young minds in the Hitler Youth, we arrived at a horrific place. Following the warmth of hearth and home, the joyful sharing of food with your community, we come to a wonderful place.

Sophia rejected one tradition. For this act of love, she was killed.

Our act of love is modest—a simple recipe from our hearts—but we see it as a celebration of those traditions that bring us together. We imagine Sophie, alive and well, taking joy in her homeland's beautiful traditions.

Sophie Scholl

Cutout cookies are a staple of German culture—the kind of tradition we can get behind! Christmas markets full of cozy tables stacked with cutout spice cookies and steaming mugs of mulled wine: the scene reflects a Germany of community, of compassion and joy.

Like us, cookie dough is changeable, rolled and rerolled again and again, shaped and reshaped. We like these cookies slightly thicker than normal, made with spelt flour, but you can sub out for another preferred flour. We top them with a rosewater glaze in remembrance of our favorite White Rose and chopped pistachios for color and crunch.

RECIPE

2 ½ cups spelt flour (or all-purpose flour)
¾ cup sugar
¼ teaspoon sea salt
16 tablespoons unsalted butter, cut into ½-inch pieces and
      at room temperature
2 tablespoons cream cheese, at room temperature
1 teaspoon vanilla extract (see recipe on page 191 for a homemade version)
1 teaspoon rose water (or almond extract)

SWEET

- Combine the flour, sugar, and salt in the bowl of a standing mixer fitted with a paddle attachment. Set the mixer to low, and add the butter chunks one at a time, mixing well to incorporate all the butter; the dough will look slightly wet. Add the cream cheese, vanilla extract, and rose water, and mix well for 30 more seconds to incorporate.

- Knead the dough by hand in the bowl two or three times to bring it all together into one cohesive mass. Divide the dough into two pieces, form each into a disk shape, and wrap in plastic wrap. Refrigerate the dough to firm it up, at least 30 minutes.

- Preheat the oven to 375°F, and line baking sheets with parchment paper.

- Roll the first disk of dough between two pieces of parchment paper until it reaches ¼-inch thick. Peel off the top layer of parchment paper, and cut out desired shapes. Place the cutout cookies on a lined baking sheet with at least 1 inch of space between cookies. Bake one sheet at a time until cookies are light golden in color, about 10 minutes (depending on the cutout size). Dough scraps can be patted together, chilled, and rolled again. Let the cookies cool on the sheet for a couple of minutes before transferring to a wire rack. Allow to cool completely before glazing.

Sophie Scholl

ROSE WATER ICING

2 cups confectioners' sugar
1 teaspoon cream cheese, at room temperature
2 ½–3 tablespoons milk
2 teaspoons rose water
Pink food coloring or beet juice, as desired (optional)
¼ cup chopped pistachios (optional as garnish)
Edible fresh or dried rose petals (optional as garnish)

- Whisk sugar, cream cheese, milk, rose water, and coloring together in a bowl until smooth and well combined.

- Glaze the cookies by using the back of a spoon to drizzle or spread approximately 1 teaspoon of glaze onto each cooled cookie. Top with pistachio pieces and edible rose petals if desired. Allow to set for 30 minutes before serving.

RECIPE PAIRING IDEA

Cookies love the company of other sweets. Serve these cookies along with Angela Davis's Spiced Molasses Cake with Crunchy Lemon Glaze (page 170) and the Mirabal Sisters' Sweet, Salty, and Spicy Popcorn (page 166), and get these freedom fighters at the table together.

SWEET

The Question at the Table

What issues (social or personal) were occupying your mind most at twenty-one years old? If you're not twenty-one yet, what would you like to be engaged in?

JUDY CHICAGO

USA, 1939–

"Because men have a history, it is difficult for them to imagine what it is like to grow up without one, or the sense of personal expansion that comes from discovering that we women have a worthy heritage."

If you studied art history in college, you definitely saw a picture of it. Judy Chicago's *The Dinner Party* (1979), a large-scale art installation celebrating and teaching women's history through elaborate, evocative dinner settings, forming the symbolic female shape of a triangle. Each setting in this ceremonial banquet varies in height, symbolizing the constant rise and fall of women's rights throughout history. Thirty-seven of the thirty-nine plates depict a brightly colored, stylized vulva, shining a brilliant light on the hidden but ever powerful parts of female anatomy.

When envisioning how *The Dinner Party* would come to life, Judy explored the context of tables, particularly how they were portrayed in art. Leonardo da Vinci's *The Last Supper* immediately came to mind. Chicago described, "I became amused by the notion of doing a sort of reinterpretation of that all-male event from the point of view of those who had traditionally been expected to prepare the food, then silently disappear from the picture or, in this case, from the picture plane."

Today, this piece stands on permanent display at the Brooklyn Museum, but at the time of *The Dinner Party*'s unveiling, it was torn to shreds by the press. Major newspapers, art reviewers, and even members of Congress took to their soapboxes to disagree and diminish the sentiment of Judy's work.

The criticism only fueled Judy's artistic flame. Her voice has continued to ring loud and clear throughout her long and prolific career. Her work combines traditional women's crafts with industrial elements including welding and pyrotechnics, obliterating stereotypes about what *women's art* is. Even her name—earned due to her inescapable Chicago accent—is a statement of intent, an emancipation from a system that defines women by their relationships with men.

A feisty individualist, for sure, but Judy has never been content to work alone. With the help of her artist and academic peers, she founded the first two feminist art programs at major universities, helping to shape the feminist art movement of the 1970s. *The Dinner Party*, her most enduring work, was itself a monumental collaborative project combining the volunteer work of hundreds of women—each of whom helped shape Judy's vision. Other notable art projects by Chicago include *International Honor Quilt*, *Birth Project*, *PowerPlay*, and *Holocaust Project*.

Judy has labored for over five decades, using art as a vessel for intellectual transformation and social change. She is an artist, activist, educator, writer, and humanist focused on a woman's right to freedom of expression.

"I am trying to make art that relates to the deepest and most mythic concerns of humankind, and I believe that, at this moment of history, feminism is humanism."

Ginger Brûléed Grapefruit

YIELD: 4–6 SERVINGS

Judy Chicago is quite possibly our favorite ginger. With her fiery red, pink, or orange hair (depending on the day), colorful outfits, and feisty track record, she was an easy choice for our book.

As these two grapefruit halves sat on our plate, bubbling with ginger caramel and dolloped with fresh cream, we couldn't help but make out a beautiful bosom staring back at us. We knew immediately that Judy Chicago's recipe had been found. This tangy, sweet, sour, and slightly spicy mix of ingredients is topped with coconut yogurt or fresh whipped cream (or anything in the ballpark; get creative!).

This is the perfect option for your brunch buffet, tea party, dessert table—or possibly even *the* dinner party.

RECIPE

3 ruby grapefruits, halved
½ cup raw sugar (also known as turbinado sugar)
1 tablespoon runny honey
1 tablespoon crystalized ginger, finely chopped
¼ teaspoon ground ginger
⅛ teaspoon ground cardamom
Pinch of sea salt
Fresh whipped cream, Greek yogurt, or coconut yogurt to top

- Set oven to broil with the oven rack in the upper half of the oven.

- Trim away a thin layer off the bottom of each grapefruit half so they will sit flat on a tray and plate. Run a small serrated knife between the grapefruit flesh and the pith,

Judy Chicago

then run the knife along the segments from center to outer edge. Line the halves up on a sheet tray.

- Combine the sugar, honey, crystalized and ground ginger, cardamom, and salt in a small bowl, and mix together well with your hands. Pile approximately 2 tablespoons of the spiced sugar mixture on top of each grapefruit half. Broil on high for 4 to 5 minutes or until caramelized, bubbling, and slightly golden. Watch them closely!

- Once cooled for just a minute or two, top each grapefruit half with a dollop of fresh whipped cream or choice of yogurt.

RECIPE PAIRING IDEA

This dish is a fantastic breakfast or dessert to end a meal. Maybe you serve Megan Rapinoe's Winning Breakfast Sandwich (page 70) alongside as the perfect breakfast spread. Or you can finish off a dinner of Frida Kahlo's Self-Illustrated Tortilla Soup (page 82) and discuss all the brave artists of the world.

SWEET

The Question at the Table

Who would you invite to your dream dinner party? Your guest list can include anyone from any time period and can be as intimate or large scale as you please.

ARETHA FRANKLIN

USA, 1942–2018

> "We all require and want respect,
> man or woman, Black or white.
> It's our basic human right."

Eighteen Grammy wins, forty-three nominations, 112 charted Billboard singles. Aretha Franklin is one of the bestselling music artists of all time, combining vibrant, four-octave-spanning vocals with enough passion for five or six equally talented—as if that were possible—singers. She became the first woman inducted into the Rock and Roll Hall of Fame, and *Rolling Stone* ranked her the greatest singer of all time.

It's not like her fate was written in the stars though. Aretha grew up with a large family in a small house in Detroit. Her mother died before her tenth birthday, and she had two children of her own before her fifteenth birthday.

Still, singing was in Aretha's blood. Her mother had been an accomplished singer and pianist, and Aretha often sang gospel at her minister father's church. When she was eighteen, her first single reached number 10 on the Billboard charts. By the close of the 1960s—after releasing over a dozen studio albums—people were calling her the Queen of Soul.

Those are important touchstones of a decades-long career, but what's more important is this: RESPECT. Aretha not only achieved her dream of becoming a musical sensation, she stood out in the civil rights movement with that seven-letter anthem. In that one foot-stomping, ass-shaking single, she sent her own personal, undeniable message to the world: *I'm* telling you what respect looks like, not the other way around.

Peace, gender equality, racial justice—Aretha Franklin fought for them all. She even tried to post bail for another woman in these pages, Angela Davis, when she was jailed in 1970. Aretha did it despite the threat it caused to her career and despite the words of her father.

"My daddy says I don't know what I'm doing. Well, I respect him, of course, but I'm going to stick by my beliefs. Angela Davis must go free. Black people will be free. I've been locked up...and I know you got to disturb the peace when you can't get no peace."

Peaches and Biscuits

YIELD: 4–6 SERVINGS

R-E-S-Peach-E-C-T.

The Queen of Soul loved Southern comfort foods—as we all should. In celebration of her good taste, we give you the world's most perfect combination: peaches and biscuits.

It doesn't get much better than tender buttermilk biscuit dough dropped by the heavy spoonful onto a dreamy mix of sweetened fruit. Our favorite way to make this dish is in a heavy cast iron skillet. A great dessert to end a summer meal or (and this is our favorite way to eat it) for breakfast the next morning. Regardless of when you eat it, don't forget to pour heavy cream over the top just before you dive in.

No peaches? No problem! They can easily be substituted for blackberries, raspberries, pitted cherries, rhubarb and strawberries, or nectarines and blueberries.

PEACHES

2 pounds fresh peaches, peeled and sliced into ½-inch wedges
½ cup sugar
3 tablespoons all-purpose flour
½ teaspoon freshly grated nutmeg
Zest from one lemon
Pinch of sea salt

- Combine all ingredients in a large bowl, and let sit for a few minutes while you prepare the biscuits.

DROP BISCUITS

1 cup all-purpose flour
¼ cup whole wheat flour
¼ cup sugar, plus 1 tablespoon for sprinkling
1 ½ teaspoons baking powder
¼ teaspoon baking soda
¼ teaspoon of sea salt
8 tablespoons cold unsalted butter, cut into small cubes
½ cup and 2 tablespoons cold buttermilk
1 tablespoon runny honey
2 tablespoons milk
1 ½ cups cold heavy cream

- Preheat the oven to 350°F.

- Combine the flours, sugar, baking powder, baking soda, and salt in the bowl of a stand mixer. Add the cold cubed butter a few cubes at a time with the motor running on low, until the mixture is sandy with butter pieces the size of peas. (Alternatively, you can do this step by hand with a pastry cutter or two forks.)

- Slowly add the cold buttermilk and honey with the motor running, until the mixture just comes together.

- Pour the peach mixture into a deep 9-inch pan or a 10-inch cast iron skillet. Drop biscuit dough in 6 to 10 heaps (about ¼ cup each, depending on pan shape and ideal biscuit size) onto the peaches. Brush the biscuits with milk and sprinkle with sugar. Bake the peaches and biscuits on a rack in the lower half of the oven for 30 minutes or until the tops are a light golden brown and the peaches are bubbling below.

- Let cool for 15 minutes before digging in. Spoon onto plates, and drizzle with heavy cream.

RECIPE PAIRING IDEA

Like we mentioned before, we love this dish for breakfast the day after it's made. If you plan to cozy up to this after the sun rises, then consider inviting Marsha P. Johnson and her Golden Baked Eggs (page 76) as well. Or you can finish the meal of Zitkala-Sa's Skillet Maize with Spicy Cherry Tomato Salsa (page 62) with Aretha's sweet number.

The Question at the Table

When was a time you felt genuinely respected by others?

THE MIRABAL SISTERS

DOMINICAN REPUBLIC, 1924/27/35–1960

> Trujillo asked Minerva, "And what if I send
> my subjects to conquer you?" She responded,
> "And what if I conquer your subjects?"

Let's be frank. Being a woman with principles—especially among men who would have you sit and be quiet—can be a dangerous position. Not all the lives of courageous women end well. Even as their stories inspire us, we are aware of how easily our heroes can be silenced.

The Mirabal Sisters, for instance: three women born into a middle-class Dominican Republic family in the 1920s and 1930s. They grew up during the reign of dictator Rafael Trujillo—or, as he was known, El Jefe. Trujillo's three decades in power were defined by corrupt totalitarianism, state-sponsored terrorism, political uncertainty and poverty throughout the country, and the massacre of thousands. The Mirabal Sisters—Patria, Minerva, and María Teresa—and their husbands became leaders and symbols of anti-Trujillo resistance. They boldly rose in defiance against this powerful stronghold, and through their initiatives, many others found the strength to follow suit. All six were jailed multiple times for their involvement in various protests and movements.

On their own, Patria, Minerva, and María Teresa formed one of the most kickass-named groups in the herstory of the world—Las Mariposas ("The Butterflies").

The butterfly symbolizes not only great beauty but strength through change. Like the past itself, the process of metamorphosis is still shrouded in mystery. From the safe womb of her chrysalis, the caterpillar undergoes one of the greatest natural feats, becoming an almost entirely new creature in only a handful of days. As she emerges, her billowing wings take her far from her once-land-bound life into the freedom of the skies. Las Mariposas, then, could not be a more fitting name for the brave Mirabal sisters: they emerged new, bright, and powerful for one single purpose—freedom.

Not satisfied with distributing pamphlets of the many people Trujillo had ordered killed, Las Mariposas gathered guns and materials for bomb-making to use when the revolution occurred.

Despite stateside and international pressure, Trujillo would not brook such behavior, responding with violence. On November 25, 1960, while traveling home from visiting their imprisoned husbands, the Mirabal Sisters were attacked by Trujillo's secret police. They and their driver were taken out, strangled, and clubbed to death. In an attempt to cover up the murders, their bodies were placed back into the vehicle and pushed over a cliff.

The cover-up failed. Word of the sisters' deaths reached every corner of the Dominican Republic. Six months later, Trujillo fell to an assassin's bullet—an event made possible, many historians believe, by the courage of the Mirabal Sisters. Every year on the anniversary of the sisters' murders, the United Nations celebrates the International Day for the Elimination of Violence against Women. We look to the sky, hoping to spot the spread wings of Las Mariposas, the symbol of liberty for all.

Sweet, Salty, and Spicy Popcorn

YIELD: 4–6 SERVINGS

When we considered the Mirabal Sisters' vitality, their inconceivable bravery in the face of powers much greater than their own, we pictured the ideal food. Something glorious in celebration of lives lived on such a grand—some might even say *cinematic*—scale.

Popcorn, we said to ourselves. But it must be respectful of Latinx cultures, an appropriate homage. Thus, the three main flavor profiles that stand out in the recipe—brown butter, maple syrup, and coconut—make this dish a close flavor sister to the iconic tres leches cake of Central America. How could we not pair these three flavors with these three memorable sisters?

Adjust the salt and cayenne to your personal taste for that perfect sweet, salty, and spicy balance.

RECIPE

⅓ cup popcorn kernels
¼ cup salted butter
2 tablespoons maple syrup
2 tablespoons coconut butter (see note below recipe)
Pinch of sea salt
Pinch of cayenne (optional, but suggested)
¼ teaspoon baking soda

- Preheat the oven to 210°F.

- Have all of your ingredients ready and measured out, as the following process goes quickly!

- Pop the kernels in an air popper (preferred) or whatever method is best for you. Try to separate the popped from unpopped kernels. Lay the popcorn out on a lined baking sheet.

- Melt the butter in a medium-sized saucepan over low heat, keeping an eye on it until it browns. You want to see and smell nuttiness in the color and scent, about 4 to 5 minutes. Whisk in the maple syrup, taking caution as the steam is very hot. Cook for 2 more minutes, then remove from the heat. Add the coconut butter, salt, and cayenne (if you're feeling daring). Stir with a wooden spoon until well combined. Quickly add the baking soda, and stir vigorously for a moment; the mixture will begin to rise up and look almost foamy. Pour the maple mixture over the popcorn on the tray. Use the wooden spoon to mix the popcorn around as you go. Try to get the coated popcorn into a single layer on the tray.

- Bake the popcorn for 3 minutes, then stir the mixture around a bit, and bake for 3 more minutes. You'll see that the color of the maple butter will become slightly darker, and the baking will help it set and eliminate more moisture.

- Let the popcorn cool before diving in for fistfuls.

NOTE: *Coconut butter may seem like a new and unique ingredient to some, but It is definitely worth seeking out for the ultimate creamy dreamy-coconutty flavor that this recipe calls for. Also, coconut butter has a long shelf life and makes a delicious addition to any smoothie!*

> ### RECIPE PAIRING IDEA
> Pop some Mirabal Sisters corn and consider heating up some of Amelia Earhart's Rich Hot Chocolate (page 202) or mixing Rupi Kaur's Summer Shrub (page 208) over ginger beer and ice for the ultimate movie-watching accessories.

The Question at the Table

If you had to right an injustice in your community, what two individuals would you choose to round out your Las Mariposas crew of three?

ANGELA DAVIS

USA, 1944–

> "You have to act as if it were possible to radically transform the world. And you have to do it all the time."

Sunday, September 15, 1963, Birmingham, Alabama. Nineteen-year-old Angela Davis woke up to the news. A bomb—nineteen sticks of dynamite planted by the Ku Klux Klan—had exploded on the steps of the Sixteenth Street Baptist Church, killing Addie Mae Collins, Cynthia Wesley, Carole Robertson, and Carol Denise McNair.

The four girls were Angela's friends. No one would be prosecuted for the crime for another fourteen years.

"We knew that the role of the police was to protect white supremacy," Angela later said.

She knew too much about white supremacy, in fact, and from too young an age. She'd grown up in the Jim Crow–era South, America's own apartheid. Her neighborhood was known as Dynamite Hill, a grisly nickname if there ever was one—bombings of Black homes and businesses were that common.

Her mother refused to let Angela grow up seeing only division though. She told Angela that things could change, that Angela could be a part of that change. She studied French at Brandeis University and philosophy at the University of Frankfurt in West Germany, embracing Marxism and far-left political ideologies.

Due to her politics, she became an intimidating figure to white folks—she was a *radical*, the angry Black woman with the large Afro. Following an infamous shootout at the Marin County

Courthouse by someone using a gun registered to Davis, she was added to the FBI's Most Wanted List.

Following her arrest, the globe took up the chant, "Free Angela!" Enraged over her unjust treatment, Angela spent eighteen months in jail before being acquitted of all charges.

Despite winning her own freedom, the anger never quite faded. For more than fifty years, Angela has been an uncompromising and relentless political activist involved in local and global struggles for human rights. She's worked harder than anyone to transform our minds and our systems. She is, by far, one of the most influential voices of the last century.

Angela, thank you for your courage. Thank you for your intellect. Thank you for your anger. And thank you for your activism.

Spiced Molasses Cake with Crunchy Lemon Glaze

YIELD: 8–10 SERVINGS

Diving into one of Angela Davis's books is a reality-altering experience—you are engaged with the history of oppression, not just for displaced Africans but for all marginalized people. You also become aware of your own longing for freedom, for everyone's freedom.

Though Angela is a skilled writer, there's no hiding her ferocity—and why would she hide that anyway?

Inspired by that fire, we pair Angela's legacy with a recipe that is flavor-forward, bold, dramatically crisp on the outside, but tender on the inside: a spiced molasses cake with a crunchy lemon glaze. It's spiced with fresh ginger, giving it that heat, and rounded out with dark cocoa.

We chose to bake this cake as a gorgeous Bundt. If you haven't invested in a Bundt pan yet, now is the time to do it! We love them so much that we've even included another Bundt recipe in this book (turn back several pages for Hedy Lemar and her Vibrant Lemon Poppy Seed Bundt Cake).

This spicy molasses cake is truly the kind of cake you tell stories over. Get your hands on a copy of one of Angela's books (we recommend *Women, Race & Class* as a good place to start), and keep the conversation going.

RECIPE

1 tablespoon unsalted butter, melted
2 cups and 1 tablespoon all-purpose flour, divided
¼ cup cocoa powder
¾ teaspoon cinnamon
¼ teaspoon ground cloves
¼ teaspoon ground ginger
¼ teaspoon sea salt
¾ cup sugar
¾ cup molasses
¾ cup neutral oil
3 ounces fresh ginger root
¾ cup boiling water
2 teaspoons baking soda
2 eggs, lightly beaten

- Preheat the oven to 325°F.

- Combine the melted butter and 1 tablespoon flour to form a paste. Using a pastry brush, apply the paste to all the curves of your Bundt pan.

- Combine the remaining flour, cocoa, spices, and salt in a medium bowl. Whisk and set aside.

- Combine the sugar, molasses, and oil in a large bowl. Peel the ginger root by scraping the skin off with a side of a spoon, and grate with a microplane over the molasses mixture. Whisk well until emulsified; it may take a minute or two.

- Pour the boiling water into a liquid measuring cup, and stir in the baking soda. Pour this into the molasses mixture, and whisk well. The mixture will get foamy quickly.

Angela Davis

- Add the flour mixture, and mix gently but consistently in the same direction to eliminate lumps, until almost combined. Add the beaten eggs, and continue mixing until the batter comes together. Don't overmix, or the batter will be tough and dense.

- Pour the batter into the prepared cake pan, and bake for 1 hour, or until a cake tester comes out clean.

CRUNCHY LEMON GLAZE

2–3 tablespoons lemon juice
⅓ cup white granulated sugar
1 cup confectioners' sugar
¼ cup candied ginger
Zest of 1 lemon

- Whisk the lemon juice, granulated sugar, and confectioners' sugar together in a bowl.

- When the cake has cooled for about 10 to 15 minutes, invert from the Bundt pan, and liberally brush the glaze onto the cake. Sprinkle candied ginger and lemon zest on the glazed cake before it dries.

- Allow the cake to cool completely before slicing.

> ### RECIPE PAIRING IDEA
> Serve slices of this cake to end a meal of Frida Kahlo's Self-Illustrated Tortilla Soup (page 82) or alongside Amelia Earhart's Rich Hot Chocolate (page 202) to snack on while diving deep into one of Angela's incredible books.

The Question at the Table

Were there any systems or ideas you inherited in your personal life that you have worked to challenge?

JANE GOODALL

ENGLAND, 1934–

> "Every individual makes a difference. We cannot live through a single day without making an impact on the world around us. And we all have free choice—what sort of difference do we want to make?"

We're sure you're tough, but are you Jane Goodall tough?

Because *tough* is walking into a Tanzanian jungle without extensive training and becoming neighbors with chimps—creatures whose strength far eclipse yours. *Tough* is trying to live alongside those creatures, whose culture is based on unpredictable alliances, hierarchies of authority you can't begin to imagine.

Now, imagine doing that for *six decades*.

Tough, it's safe to say, isn't even the word. We prefer...*ferociously gentle*?

Jane's fascination with African animals started early. In 1957, at the age of twenty-three, she went to Kenya and began searching for ways to study animals. By 1960—with no formal degree—she was studying chimps at Gombe National Park in Tanzania. With only a pair of binoculars, a notebook, and a burning curiosity, she ventured deep into the wilds of the jungle. For years, she lived as a neighbor to the chimpanzees, witnessing their lives in a new way, quietly and humbly. Her findings were groundbreaking to researchers all over the world. She would go on to receive a PhD in animal behavior from Newnham College,

Cambridge—studying for a PhD without first receiving a bachelor's degree. In 1977, she realized the best help she could give her dear friends, the chimpanzees, was to leave them. She founded the Jane Goodall Institute (JGI), which provided the ongoing support that the primates most needed. Today, Dr. Goodall's visionary efforts have established community-centered conservation and grassroots developmental programs around the world.

Throughout her illustrious career, Jane has redefined the interconnection of animals, humans, and Mother Earth. Sure, she didn't always follow the rules—for which she's been criticized. But Jane broke the mold and came away a stronger, more compassionate advocate for the animals she dedicated her life to.

Now in her eighties, Jane remains at the forefront of every major development in our understanding of primate culture and evolution. She has been named a Messenger of Peace by the United Nations and continues to be a tireless voice in areas of human rights, poverty eradication, community development, peace and conflict resolution, disarmament, and environmentalism. Few people in history have had a larger impact on the future of our environment.

Jane Goodall

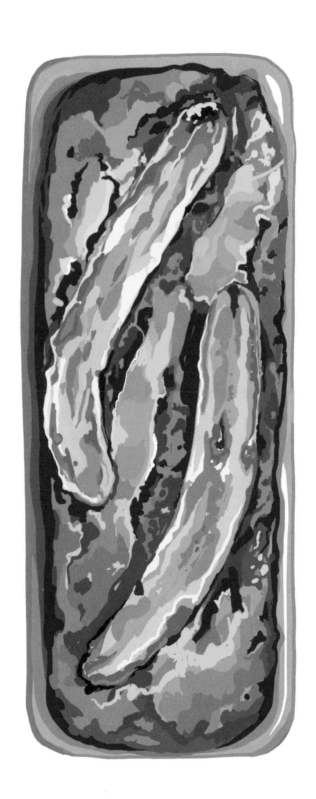

Palm Sugar Banana Bread

YIELD: 8–10 SERVINGS

Jane Goodall gleefully crossed the traditional boundaries between researcher and subject. Instead of assigning her primate subjects numbers, she named them: Fifi, Flo, and David Greybeard were just a few of the chimpanzees that she set out to befriend.

Bananas were a great icebreaker. (See? You thought we were just being lazy—*banana bread* for chimps!) The delicious treat allowed Jane to develop a strong bond and to record behavior that had never been recorded before.

This is not your average banana bread. Four well-ripened bananas give this baked loaf its traditional moist allure, while the caramel-colored coconut palm sugar and the addition of melted butter make it an instant friend to all bananas Foster lovers. Invite some best buds to your camp, and raise a slice to the amazing Jane Goodall!

RECIPE

4 medium-sized very ripe bananas (it is important that the stems are not green at all but mostly brown), divided

½ cup unsalted butter, melted, plus more for the pan

¾ cup and 3 tablespoons coconut palm sugar (or coconut sugar or dark brown sugar), divided

1 ½ teaspoon vanilla extract (see recipe on page 191 for a homemade version)

2 eggs

2 cups all-purpose flour

1 teaspoon baking powder

½ teaspoon baking soda

½ teaspoon sea salt

½ teaspoon ground ginger

¼ teaspoon ground nutmeg

4 ounces chopped dark chocolate (optional)

Jane Goodall

- Preheat the oven to 350°F. Butter the bottom and sides of a 9-by-5-inch loaf pan, and line with a parchment paper sling.

- Mash three of the bananas really well in a large bowl, then add the melted butter, palm sugar, vanilla, and eggs. Stir well.

- Whisk together the flour, baking powder, baking soda, salt, and spices in a medium bowl.

- Add the dry mixture and the chopped chocolate to the large bowl with the banana mixture. Stir to combine, but do not overmix (or you will get tough "tunneling" throughout your bread—pro tip!).

- Pour the batter into the prepared pan. Halve the remaining banana lengthwise, and place on top of the batter. Sprinkle with the remaining 3 tablespoons of coconut palm sugar.

- Bake for 45 to 60 minutes, or until a cake tester comes out clean.

- Allow to cool for 15 minutes before pulling from the pan or cutting.

RECIPE PAIRING IDEA

This banana bread is so versatile: it could be breakfast, a gift to your neighbor, or even just the everyday cake you treat yourself with. Consider inviting Ruth Coker Burks's Rainbow Salad (page 14) to lunch or Sophie Scholl's White Rose Butter Cookies (page 146) to your bake sale. Any way you pair it, all will be in good company with banana bread and Jane Goodall.

The Question at the Table

Have you had a relationship with an animal that changed you?

CLAUDETTE COLVIN

USA, 1939–

"I felt like Sojourner Truth was pushing down on one shoulder and Harriet Tubman was pushing down on the other—saying, 'Sit down girl!' I was glued to my seat."

We're sure you've heard of Rosa Parks, who refused to move to the back of the bus and give up her seat to a white person in Montgomery, Alabama. With this infamous act, the Montgomery Bus Boycott ignited and set off revolutionary change for a segregated America.

But it's unlikely you've heard of Claudette Colvin. As advocates for racial justice, we should all know Claudette's name and what she stood—rather, *sat*—for.

On March 2, 1955, nine months before Rosa Parks's famous act of civil disobedience, fifteen-year-old Claudette refused to give up her seat on another Montgomery, Alabama, bus. "It's my constitutional right to sit here as much as that lady," she said. "I paid my fare. It's my constitutional right."

Claudette was only a student at the time. She'd heard of brave Black women who courageously stepped out of line (specifically Tubman and Truth), challenging racial inequality, but the constant reminder of her place in a white world pressed on her shoulders. Black citizens couldn't sit at the bar in a restaurant. They couldn't use the same restroom as white citizens. Even the act of trying on a pair of shoes meant that Claudette had to trace her foot on a paper bag and bring it to the shoe store in order to match her size. So many daily obstructions, the weight of every macro- and microaggression, fueled her righteous anger to stay seated when told to stand.

Unlike Rosa, Claudette had not been trained in civil disobedience. She had her pride. She knew right from wrong: "I had stood up for our rights. I had done something a lot of adults hadn't done."

The NAACP considered using Claudette's case to challenge the state's segregation laws but ultimately decided against it, shifting their focus to Rosa. Claudette was too young, too dark complexioned. Added to that, she had become pregnant. Regardless, following 1956's *Browder v. Gayle*, the Supreme Court ruled Montgomery's segregated bus system unconstitutional—a direct result of Claudette's refusal to give up her place.

Like so many history-changing women before her, Claudette hasn't received nearly her fair share of recognition. Having come to terms with her place in history, however, she has said, "I don't think there's room for any more icons."

Respectfully, we disagree.

Travel Tea Cake with Zucchini, Carrot, and Apple

YIELD: 8–10 SERVINGS

We won't forget Claudette. Her courage and trust in herself gives us pause. At only fifteen, she knew she could trust her intuition and where it would lead. It led her into some deep discomfort, being yelled at, physically manhandled, and disrespected when she chose to sit instead of walk. But sometimes, it's the uncomfortable moments that pave the way for big change. And Claudette was truly at the forefront of a monumental shift.

We thought about giving you all a complex, multistep recipe that would stretch your limits and maybe even make you a little uncomfortable (obviously nothing compared to fighting racial injustice!), but we are going to let the legacy of Claudette's heroic act do the heavy lifting.

Not only is this a simple, one-bowl wonder of a cake, it's also incredibly quick to throw together and hard to mess up. Make note that you can alter the proportions to make up your two and a half cups of fruit and veg required: you only have half an apple, a chunk of zucchini, and a few carrots? No problem! You can make this cake with any combination of the three or even just two of them.

This cake travels well, so once it's cooled, pack it up alongside Claudette's story and take it to the streets. Both deserve to be shared.

RECIPE

1 cup chopped nuts (pecans or walnuts)

2 cups mix of carrot, apple, and zucchini, grated

2 eggs

1 cup all-purpose flour

¾ cup sugar, plus more for topping

½ cup golden raisins, finely chopped

½ cup whole wheat flour

½ cup neutral oil

2 teaspoons ground cinnamon

2 teaspoons ground flax seeds

1 ½ teaspoons baking soda

1 teaspoon baking powder

1 teaspoon sea salt

1 teaspoon vanilla extract (see recipe on page 191 for a homemade version)

½ teaspoon freshly ground nutmeg

Zest of 1 organic orange

- Preheat the oven to 350°F. Oil the bottom and sides of a 9-by-5-inch loaf pan, and line with a parchment paper sling.

- Place the nuts on a baking sheet and toast for approximately 7 minutes. Allow them to cool and then chop.

- Put everything into a large bowl, and mix together just until combined. Really. Just add it all in no special order, and mix it up. Use your hands if you want to!

- Pour the batter into the loaf pan, and sprinkle the top with a couple of tablespoons of sugar. This gives the top a nice crunch.

- Bake for 50 to 60 minutes or until a cake tester comes out clean.

- Allow to cool for at least 15 minutes before cutting off a chunk.

RECIPE PAIRING IDEA

The great thing about a cake this style (quick breads in general) is really its portability. Your next holiday party? Bring Claudette's cake and Sophie Scholl's White Rose Butter Cookies (page 146). Invited to a brunch? Bring Claudette's cake and Marsha P. Johnson's Golden Baked Eggs (page 76).

SWEET

The Question at the Table

When was a time that you had a strong feeling in your gut, an angel on your shoulder, or a voice in the back of your head that told you to move forward, stay put, or make change?

Claudette Colvin

KATRÍN JAKOBSDÓTTIR

ICELAND, 1976–

> "My problem in my life—and also my fortune—is to always say yes. When people ask me to do interesting things, I tend to do them."

She dreamed of being a surgeon or a rock star. Iceland had other plans for her. Iceland needed her to be a leader, so Katrín Jakobsdóttir stepped up, and in 2017, she became one of the youngest women to lead a European country.

The thing is, Katrín likes to say yes—to leadership, to motherhood, and even to a now-viral 1996 music video where she played a femme fatale running around the streets of Reykjavík. But don't let this fool you into thinking she's going with the flow. Under her leadership, Iceland's government rolled out one of the strongest equal-pay legislations in the world while tackling key issues like universal child care and shared parental leave.

A mother of three, Katrín is the perfect example of how professional women benefit from child care and parental leave: she wouldn't have made it to her current position without laws that ensure a woman's right to live life *and* enjoy the professional opportunities men have always enjoyed. The Icelandic government understands that when women are enabled to participate more actively in the labor market and political decision-making, everyone benefits—including men, who are now able to explore the domestic world, raising their children.

"The best decisions are made with both men and women at the table," Katrín said.

So it's no surprise the World Economic Forum ranked Iceland as the best country to be a woman. It's the work of generations of women fighting for their priorities, *our priorities*, and it's still relatively hard to see a precedent outside Iceland.

Really, where else can a woman who studied language and literature become the leader of her country?

If it's up to Katrín, the answer will soon be *everywhere*.

Wild Blueberry Streusel Cake

YIELD: 6–8 SERVINGS

This dense and crumbly treat offers you the best of both worlds—dessert *and* tomorrow's breakfast! This is a very striking, *very* blueberry-forward cake inspired many years ago while traveling around Iceland, cooking for guests in the middle of August, the sun never setting, waterfalls flowing from every mountain-lined fjord. Someone gifted us a large bag of wild Icelandic blueberries that were absolutely mind blowing.

Now, don't worry too much about finding your own fresh Icelandic blueberries. Using frozen ones allows the fruit to bleed into the dough, giving it a vibrant indigo color. We've included a homemade vanilla extract as well, and the reason is simple: it's incredibly easy to make, just vanilla beans and a bottle of vodka. (Since vodka is a profoundly important beverage in Iceland, we wanted to bring it center stage and give you a reason to love it!)

Katrín Jakobsdóttir

STREUSEL

¾ cup sugar

⅔ cup all-purpose flour

4 tablespoons unsalted butter, cold

4 tablespoons cornmeal

½ teaspoon cinnamon

Pinch of sea salt

- Combine all the ingredients in a medium-sized bowl, and blend together with your fingertips. Break up the butter and create large crumbs by occasionally squeezing some dough together in your palm. Keep in the refrigerator until ready to use.

CAKE

1 cup all-purpose flour

½ cup cornmeal

2 teaspoons baking powder

½ teaspoon sea salt

8 tablespoons unsalted butter, softened

1 cup sugar

2 eggs

1 teaspoon homemade vanilla extract (recipe below)

⅓ cup crème fraîche

Zest of 1 lemon

2 cups frozen wild blueberries, defrosted slightly

- Preheat the oven to 350°F. Butter and flour a 9-by-9-inch square cake pan or baking dish.

- Combine the flour, cornmeal, baking powder, and salt in a medium bowl, and set aside.

- Cream the butter and sugar in the bowl of a stand mixer on medium-high speed for a few minutes, until pale and fluffy. Add the eggs, one at a time, and beat to combine. Scrape down the bowl, and add the vanilla, crème fraîche, and lemon zest, followed by additions of the dry ingredients until combined, but be careful not to overmix the dough. Gently fold in the blueberries. Leave the batter to sit

- for a moment to allow the blueberries to bleed and stain the batter. Turn the batter once more with your spatula before pouring into the prepared pan and smoothing the top.

- Pile the streusel topping over the batter in craggy piles. Bake for 45 to 50 minutes or until a cake tester comes out clean.

- Serve with a dollop of whipped cream, a cup of coffee, or a shot of vodka.

VANILLA EXTRACT

1 (26-ounce) bottle vodka
8 vanilla beans

- Place the vanilla beans in the bottle of vodka. Keep in a cool, dark place, and shake or turn once a week. This is ready to use in 3 months and long beyond that. The longer it sits, the better it tastes.

NOTE: *Allow at least three months to marry flavors before using. Oh, and do yourself a favor and pick a decent vodka here. Not the top-shelf bottle, but also not that cheap stuff you drank with juice in high school. Think decent vodka that a Viking would be happy to drink with you.*

> ### RECIPE PAIRING IDEA
> This buttery cake would be perfect for finishing a summer meal of Dickey Chapelle's Potato-Crusted Salmon with Dill and Sour Cream (page 124) or tucked in next to your coffee or Amelia Earhart's Rich Hot Chocolate (page 202) for breakfast the next day.

The Question at the Table

When was the last time you said yes to a request that
took you outside your comfort zone?

Katrín Jakobsdóttir

LIZZO

USA, 1988–

"When all the dust has settled on the groundbreaking-ness, I'm going to still be doing this. I'm not going to suddenly change. I'm going to still be telling my life story through music. And if that's body positive to you, amen. That's feminist to you, amen. If that's pro-Black to you, amen. Because ma'am, I'm all of those things."

When you attend a Lizzo concert, you worship at the Church of Self-Love. At a time when social media is selling us every insecurity—be thinner, get tanner, have the time to press backyard cider while hand-stitching your own unique eco bikini line—Lizzo sells something more radical and certainly more delicious:

You are already enough.

Born Melissa Viviane Jefferson in Detroit, Lizzo first learned about music as spirituality: she sang gospel as a child. After her family moved to Houston when she was nine, she took up the flute and joined the marching band. Lizzo continued to play until halfway through her sophomore year of college, when she decided to drop out, push her flute aside, and pursue a singing career. Things were not easy. She struggled and found herself in a toxic relationship, and for a while even lived out of her car. And then, at twenty-one, her father died suddenly.

SWEET

Lizzo has lived hardship, cruelty, and heartbreak, the kind of life that discourages many from pursuing their dreams and pushes others to try that much harder. She's a hero because she preaches self-empowerment while being candid about her struggles to love herself as she is—*all* of who she is. Her willingness to address taboos and confront sexuality with frankness shocks the squares as much as it delights the rest of us.

Lizzo is *next-level* self-love—and what's best is that she *knows it*. She owns herself, wholly and completely. Take this interview with *Vogue*:

> **V:** What's a creative risk you've taken that has paid off?
> **L:** Being myself.
> **V:** What's a creative risk you've learned the most from?
> **L:** Being myself.

Anyone who knows what it's like to struggle with their identity feels a connection to Lizzo. You feel seen for who you truly are, maybe for the first time, and being seen makes it easier to love yourself.

Lizzo is everything we could possibly want her to be: loud, fun, and as real as they come, whether she's shining like a beacon of light on Twitter or twerking in a catsuit while playing the flute. She exudes love for herself, and as if that weren't enough, she unabashedly loves *you*. That's right, you. Lizzo shares her personal mantra at the end of every concert by asking each person in the audience to go home, look in the mirror, and repeat these words until they feel the truth of it throughout their bodies.

Now repeat after Lizzo...

> I LOVE YOU.
> YOU ARE BEAUTIFUL.
> AND YOU CAN DO ANYTHING.

"I really want you to say that, because I believe we can save the world if we save ourselves first."

Vegan French Toast

YIELD: 4–6 SERVINGS

In 2020, Lizzo decided to adopt a vegan lifestyle, but she's also a lover of good food. Did you know she was even tempted by the idea of becoming a professional food critic? (Us too!)

We wanted to make Lizzo something she'd love—a dish bright with nostalgia, a comfort food so crave-worthy she'd wonder how it could possibly be vegan. French toast! We've got a delicious vegan custard made with coconut milk, turmeric, and cinnamon to soak your bread of choice in.

We think Lizzo would approve of this golden fried bread topped with a cube of vegan butter (or dairy butter if you like—you do you, girl!), swimming in a sea of maple syrup.

Picture tomorrow morning: you wake up, wash your face, touch your toes for a count of ten, and look at yourself in the mirror while repeating Lizzo's mantra, then head to the kitchen to whip up this gorgeous breakfast. Self-love in a single recipe!

RECIPE

4 tablespoons cornstarch

¾ cup full-fat coconut milk

3 teaspoons maple syrup, plus more for drizzling

2 teaspoons vanilla extract (see recipe on page 191 for a homemade version)

1 teaspoon ground cinnamon

¼ teaspoon sea salt

⅛ teaspoon ground turmeric (for color)

6 to 8 soft bread slices, ¾- to 1-inch thick (challah, brioche, or thick sandwich bread works best here)

Vegan butter or vegetable oil for cooking

- Add the cornstarch and coconut milk to a low, wide bowl, and whisk well to eliminate any lumps. Add maple syrup, vanilla, cinnamon, salt, and turmeric, and whisk to combine.

- Set slices of bread into the coconut mixture, and leave to soak on each side for at least a minute or two. A dry center in your French toast is a big no-no!

- Heat a large nonstick skillet over medium heat. Melt butter or oil of choice, and swirl it around the pan. Add slices of soaked bread to the hot pan, and allow to cook until you see the edges browning. Refuse the urge to check, or you'll disturb the crisp browning that the cornstarch helps with. Flip when ready, and cook the other side equally. Continue with remaining slices.

- Top your golden stack of French toast with butter (vegan or otherwise) and a good dose (don't hold back here) of pure maple syrup.

RECIPE PAIRING IDEA

We're thinking it would be pretty amazing to have Judy Chicago's Ginger Brûléed Grapefruit (page 154) and Aretha Franklin (who just so happens to be Lizzo's idol) and her Peaches and Biscuits (page 158) at the table with Lizzo. Just replace the dairy with nondairy substitutes to keep the whole meal vegan if you'd like.

SWEET

The Question at the Table

What self-love habit do you incorporate into your daily routine? If you don't have one, what can you start doing today to show yourself that you care and that you are worth it?

AMELIA EARHART

USA, 1897–1937

> "Women must try to do things as men have tried. When they fail, their failure must be but a challenge to others."

Imagine it: the year is 1937. A woman flies fourteen thousand feet above an ocean that extends in all directions. It's just her; her navigator, Fred Noonan; and a plane only a few generations removed from the first-ever planes, dubbed by the press as a "flying laboratory." This thin-skinned tube of metal, hurtling through the sky, is certainly not the safest vehicle—one wrong move, one simple mechanical error, and all bets are off.

But instead of being afraid, she's *elated*. She *is* Amelia Earhart after all.

Born in a small Kansas town, Amelia's childhood was not unlike many others, filled with book reading and ball throwing. It wasn't until a trip to an airfield in her early twenties that her plans changed forever. She knew then and there that she wanted to fly a plane, and nothing was going to stop her. But the world told her otherwise. Women of that era did not fly planes, did not wear pants, and definitely did not live a bold life in the limelight. Amelia was no average woman, however; she doled out birth control advice and refused to take her husband's last name. Oh, and did we mention she was the first woman to fly across the Atlantic? She was only a passenger in that 1928 flight, but the world was suddenly taking notice of this intrepid and unapologetic woman.

She liked the attention but knew that most of it was just noise. Only a handful of people had the faintest clue what she was doing, how much work it took to keep a plane in the air. And they sure as hell didn't understand the risks involved. The risks or the joys.

In 1932, Amelia repeated that first transatlantic flight, this time, entirely by herself—again, the first woman to do it. After completing the dangerous journey, Amelia felt she had finally proven that women were in fact equal to men in "jobs requiring intelligence, coordination, speed, coolness, and willpower."

By 1935, she was a visiting faculty member at Purdue University and an ardent supporter of women's rights. By breaking through the thick barrier of what women *should* or *should not* do, she earned the respect of women and men alike worldwide.

In 1937, on the verge of her fortieth birthday, Amelia attempted to circumnavigate the globe. She would have been the first woman (yet again!) to do so. Over a month into her journey, Amelia's radio fell silent over the Pacific Ocean. All conspiracy theories aside, she most likely fell out of the sky to her death.

But maybe, just maybe, she pulled back the yoke and flew straight up, shattering that glass ceiling above the clouds.

Rich Hot Chocolate

YIELD: 4 SERVINGS

While embarking over the Pacific Ocean between Honolulu and California, Amelia recounted, "It was a night of stars. Above, the clouds, they hung so close it seemed I could reach out from the cockpit and touch them. And there, eight thousand feet over the sea, in a very solitary world with only the stars for company, I luxuriated in a cup of cocoa—altogether the strangest midnight lunch I can remember." What an incredible thing, flying amid the stars, alone like few before her, with only this small comfort: a thermos of steaming hot chocolate.

Food is such a powerful vehicle. The taste of mango reminds us of our first vacations. The smell of tomato soup reminds us of how it felt to be wrapped in a treasured childhood blanket. Even the sip of rich hot cocoa takes you on a journey back in time—back to Amelia, back to those times in your backyard when you imagined your own adventure. As you enjoy this treat, know that there are adventures still to come!

RECIPE

1 ¼ cups whipping cream, divided
6 ounces semisweet (60%) chocolate, chopped
3 cups whole milk
3 tablespoons sugar or maple syrup
3 tablespoons cocoa powder
¼ teaspoon fine sea salt

- Whip 1 cup of whipping cream until soft peaks form, and set aside in the fridge.

- Melt the chocolate over a double boiler, and set aside.

- Heat the milk and syrup or sugar in a pot to steaming but not bubbling or boiling. Remove from the heat, and whisk in the cocoa powder and the melted chocolate. Whisk in the remaining whipping cream and salt. Portion into mugs. Dollop the soft whipped cream onto the cups of hot chocolate. Enjoy.

RECIPE PAIRING IDEA

Hot chocolate reminds us all of those cozy fall and winter moments we look forward to each year. We imagine this comforting drink being made with your closest friends alongside a big bowl of the Mirabal Sisters' Sweet, Salty, and Spicy Popcorn (page 166). Or maybe serve it at a festive family party alongside a platter of Sophie Scholl's White Rose Butter Cookies (page 146).

The Question at the Table

Amelia once had an *aha* moment in the sky while sipping her hot chocolate. When was a time in your life that you had an *aha* moment with food?

Amelia Earhart

RUPI KAUR

"I can be intelligent. I can be beautiful. I can be every single thing. I can be multidimensional. And it's allowed."

From the moment of her birth, Rupi was exposed to poetry. Sikh scriptures are written in beautiful and flowing poetic verses—verses her mother recited to Rupi as she rocked her to sleep each night. Poetry that would sink deep into the marrow of her being.

At the age of three, Rupi emigrated with her family from Punjab, India, to her adopted land of Canada. They were seen as outsiders, speaking a language indecipherable to the people around them. Because of her broken English, Rupi was bullied until she refused to speak. She began to find her voice in art: painting and drawing. As her English improved, so did her relationship with writing. And that was when everything changed. Words had the power to heal her trauma and to take her far from the debilitating fear that had taken her voice.

Rupi started writing poetry as a private hobby, but it steadily became an extension of her will, a limb she couldn't live without.

In her early twenties, she wrote, illustrated, and self-published her first book, *Milk and Honey*. At the time, she was studying to be a lawyer; reciting poetry was a thing she did in cafés and bars in the evenings. Listeners were struck with the fire of her words and begged her for a book. Teachers told her that poetry didn't sell, that all those authors in the bookstore's poetry section are long dead. But still, her audiences begged for more. Rupi decided to do it all herself, and her first book, *Milk and Honey*, was born.

Rupi fills the reader's mind with poems of love, heartache, and womanhood. Or look to her poem "Broken English," where she recounts the trials and triumphs of being an immigrant, a woman, a soul glorying in the effort of living. And through her words, she has become a voice for the silenced and a witness to the unseen.

"I have to tell this story. If you silence me like you've silenced so many other people, then who's gonna tell it?... There's so much empty space that needs to be filled with stories like these."

Rupi Kaur

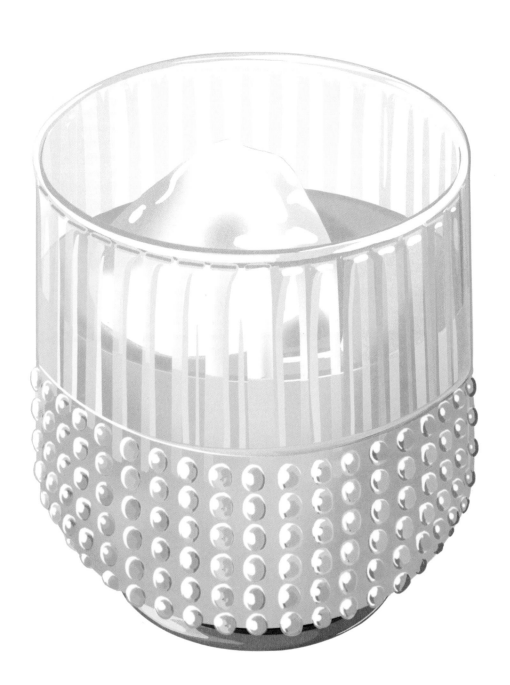

Summer Shrub

YIELD: 6–12 SERVINGS

Kaur's poetry strikes you in the mind, the body, and the soul. Her words come together like nectar, an elixir we sip slowly.

We've been sipping on her books for some time now. When the house gets quiet midday, we curl up with *Home Body*, *Milk and Honey*, or *The Sun and Her Flowers* in self-reflection.

A refreshing drink paired with her nourishing words feels just right.

We've created a shrub. New to shrubs? No problem! They are sweet and tangy elixirs to be added to drinks, with just three ingredients: fruit, sugar, and vinegar. Pour it over ice with fresh lemon and some sparkling water—or make it our favorite way, combined with a spicy ginger beer. Your senses will perk up instantly, like you're standing in a beam of sunlight.

This is a drink you learn to love in the way you learn to enjoy wine or kombucha. The vinegar gives it a tangy, probiotic effervescence. Getting the balance right can take a while, but that's part of the fun—you're the writer here, so experiment away! This recipe yields about a cup and a half, enough for six to twelve servings, depending on how strong you like your shrub.

RECIPE

1 pound pitted, unpeeled plums, apricots, or peaches
¾ cup sugar
½ cup unfiltered apple cider vinegar
Soda water or ginger beer, for the full drink

- Chop the fruit roughly, just to break it down into more manageable chunks. Place in a glass bowl or a stone mortar with the sugar. Mash the fruit to break it apart even more and encourage the juices to marry with the sugar. Cover and refrigerate for 24 hours.

- Give the fruit mixture a stir, and add the vinegar. Cover and refrigerate for another 24 hours to marry the flavors even more.

- When ready to use, stir well to make sure the sugar is dissolved, then strain using a fine mesh sieve. Be sure to press the solids to get all the juice out. Pour the shrub into a clean glass jar or glass bottle (with a pop top or cork lid).

- To prepare the drink, add 1 part shrub to 3 parts soda water or ginger beer, with a squeeze of fresh lemon. Serve over ice.

RECIPE PAIRING IDEA

This refreshing late-summer drink would be great as something to sip before dinner with Greta Thunberg's Cashew Chipotle Dip (page 34) or a bubbling warm plate of Zitkala-Sa's perfect summer meal of Skillet Maize with Spicy Cherry Tomato Salsa (page 62).

The Question at the Table

Were you ever bullied or criticized for something that eventually led you to pursue a passion or find a previously hidden strength?

Acknowledgments

WE

The seeds of this book were planted at a time when the two of us, both hazy-eyed new mothers, were craving creativity and a way to foster sisterhood. Along our three-year journey, countless individuals contributed to make this book exactly what we hoped it would be: a vehicle for bringing the stories of incredible women to conversations at the table and onward and outward. We'd like to express deep gratitude to:

The women in this book, for everything they have given us. Simply put, we have fallen in love with them. Each of them. Their stories and legacies have transformed us, inspired us, and profoundly opened our hearts. Because of them, we will never be the same.

Meg Gibbons and the incredibly talented team at Sourcebooks, for being so attentive and supportive of this vision. Just as promised in our offer letter, Meg truly was our biggest advocate at Sourcebooks.

Our trusty agents, Devon Halliday and Rob Firing, at Transatlantic Literary Agency, for believing in *A Table Set for Sisterhood*. Their knowledge, excitement, and encouragement for this book's success paved our way to publication. From the very first email, we knew we were in the best of hands.

Zack Jernigan (Ashly's brother), for not only editing our work but understanding our collective voice and fine-tuning it. He so graciously pumped his giant heart into each word he upgraded and each sentence he elevated.

Barbara Robles, for her attentive recipe testing, offering mounds of wisdom and her exquisite Virgo chef talent from her California kitchen, while the original recipes were created in Ashley's Switzerland kitchen.

Morgan Oppenheimer, for being the first person in the publishing world to take a chance on us. She pushed us, she mentored us, and without her, we're not sure this book would be here today.

Howard and Kim Schiffer, for hosting dinners and inviting deep conversations that inspired the Question at the Table portions of this book.

Keri Diamond and the Cherry Bombe team, for featuring a portion of this idea in their beautiful publication. That experience gave us fuel during a time when *A Table Set for Sisterhood* seemed like a pipe dream.

Hannah Davitian, Carrie Purcell, Junemarie Justus, Francesca Thyssen-Bornemizsa, and many others, for opening up doors for connection, letting us talk their ears off with ideas, and guiding the creation of this book with a shared excitement.

All our neighbors and friends, who let us test out recipes on them or accepted countless images and text messages in exchange for honest feedback. We relied on them heavily and are so grateful they were up for joining us on this sometimes bumpy ride.

ASHLEY

Firstly, my daughters, Mila and Solenne, for giving me a reason to create something that will last beyond my time. You two are my proudest achievements and my greatest teachers.

My dear Swiss, you have never not had my back or my heart.

My mom, for raising me to be a woman driven by passion and influenced by nature.

My dad and my brothers, for respecting women and always being a constant for me.

Kim and Peggy, wise sages who were my portals to the deep love language shared at the table.

Francesca, for wild adventures that opened my culinary eyes and kept me in love with my craft as a private chef.

My tribe of sister soul mates—sharing meals and deep conversations with them at the table has been one of my greatest joys. To a few who lent their ears and shoulders to me during this process: Aish, Emily, Barb, Ash P., Zoe, Carrie, Junemarie, Lizzie, C'est fam, Bettina, Riana, and the Mochi mamas. Thank you!

And lastly, to my partner and dear friend, Ashly. Collaborating with her on this shared dream has been an incredibly fulfilling adventure. Her talent as an artist floors me, and her empathy and dedication to the women in this book is the match that lit our collective flame. *Danke.*

ASHLY

Michael, for being my best friend and the holder of the opinions I value most. I am forever grateful for his encouragement, his patience, his critical eye, his belief in me, and his love. He is and always will be my number one.

My daughter, Zoe, for her overwhelming strength and compassion. It was only through watching her that I fully realized I was a feminist. She inspired me to write this book.

My son, Theo, for being my trusty companion. He was either growing in my belly, bouncing beside me in his BabyBjörn, or pretending to eat my food illustrations as I worked. I can feel his presence when I thumb through these pages.

My mom, for always persevering and standing her ground. While she may not call herself a feminist, she is one. She has never missed an opportunity to marvel at or to help me understand the power of womanhood. And because of her, I had no reason to doubt that power.

My dad, for being my first drawing buddy and biggest fan. I wonder how many evenings he sat in a tiny chair at my tiny table, coloring with me. Countless. His enthusiasm for me and anything I have ever done has always been a source of encouragement, not to mention beyond endearing.

My brothers, Josh, Zack, and Brennan, for being men who respect and believe in women... especially me. I was the odd one out being the only girl, but they never made me doubt my female strength. With them by my side, I always felt and still feel special. They mean more to me than words can express.

Nancy Riegelman, my mentor and friend, for seeing something in me, taking me under her wing, and pushing me to hone my skills.

My lifelong female friends, for celebrating with me, crying with me, and nourishing me. Particular shoutouts to my dear Alyson, Megan, Magi, Emily, Lene, and Marilyn, for their encouragement, shared excitement, and on-point, honest feedback as this book came together.

Ashley, my coauthor and dear friend, for trusting me enough to collaborate and create this beautiful book with me. It was her initial idea to bring our talents together, and I couldn't have asked for a better companion. She is the yin to my yang, and I am forever grateful for her.

Index

NOTE: Page numbers in *italic* refer to illustrations.